AI FANTASY KNIGHT COLORING BOOK

Hey there, I'm Jeremy Hubert Burt. I was feeling inspired and decided to use a prompt to create some 3D coloring book pages. The prompt I used was:

"Design an awe-inspiring coloring book page featuring a mighty fantasy warrior in metal armor. Against a pristine white background, use bold black lines to illustrate the warrior, emphasizing their strength and valor.

Create intricate and ornate background designs that reflect the warrior's noble lineage and heroic deeds. These designs should inspire awe and admiration.

Incorporate various shapes like engravings, swirling patterns, and symbolic emblems throughout the page, enveloping the warrior in a world of power and command. Add inspiring phrases in a powerful font to ignite courage and determination.

Outline the warrior's armor and weaponry with bold black lines, clearly defining the coloring boundaries. This allows enthusiasts to unleash their imagination and bring the warrior to life using the striking contrast of black and white.

The coloring book page offers an exhilarating journey into a realm of fantasy and adventure. It invites individuals to immerse themselves in the captivating art of coloring, providing a delightful sense of relaxation and stress relief. Embody the spirit of the noble warrior against the timeless contrast of black and white."

After creating the design, I decided to edit the levels in GIMP in greyscale image mode to give it that extra touch of depth and detail. The whole process only took me a day, and I'm really happy with the results. I even published the pages using the Sqribble ebook maker, which was super easy to use. Check out the link if you want to Publish Your eBook: https://bit.ly/3nVzjvK.

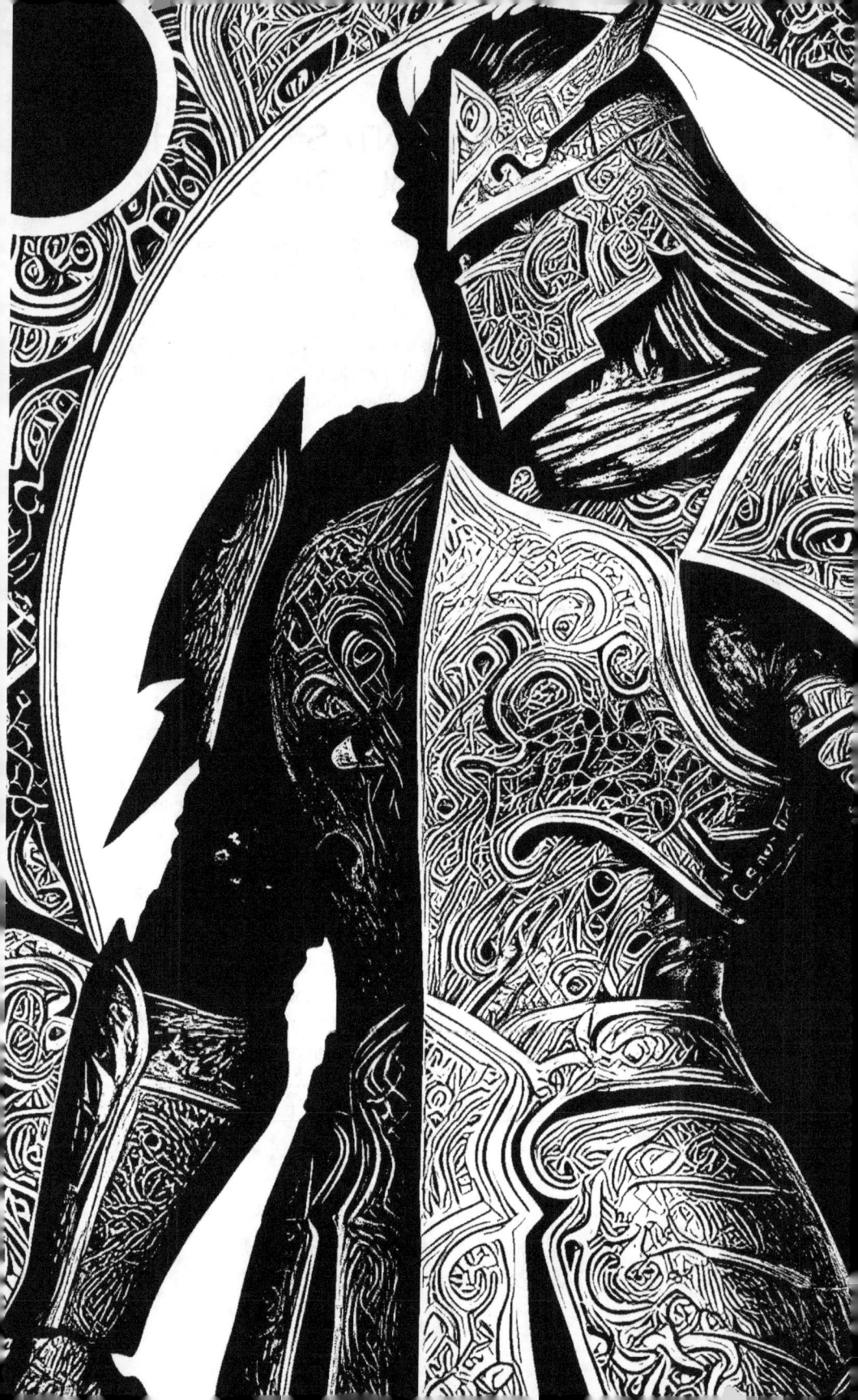

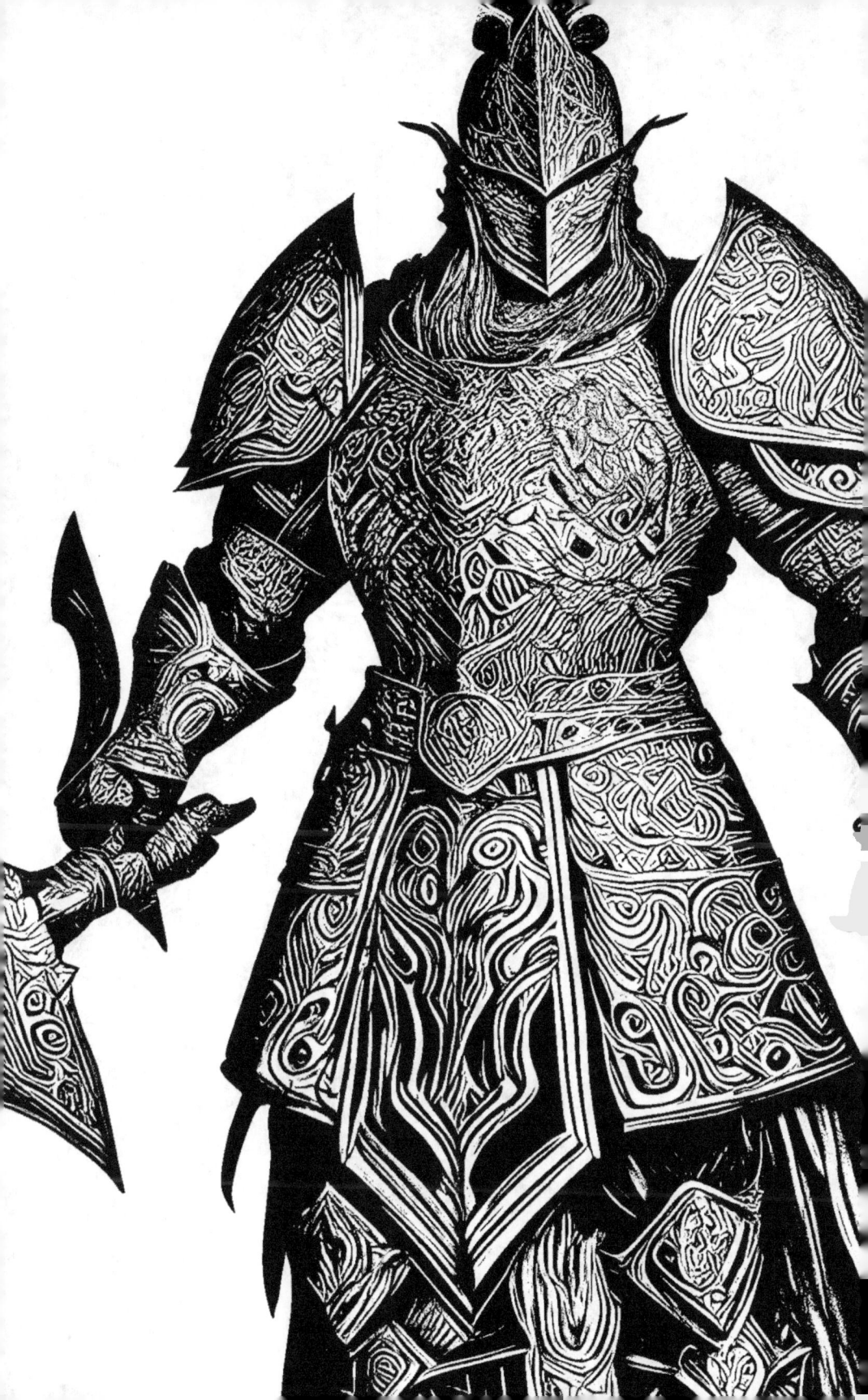

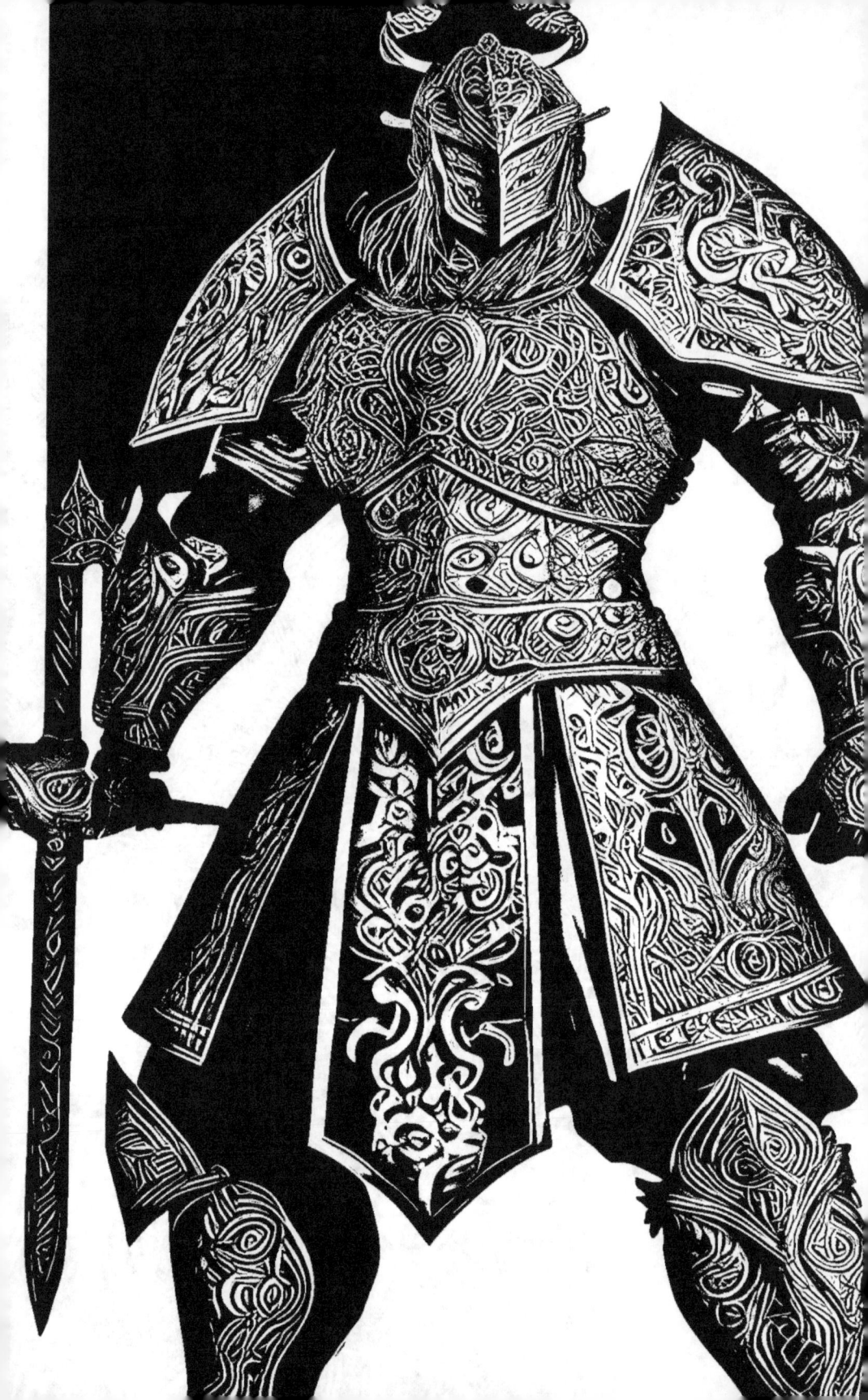

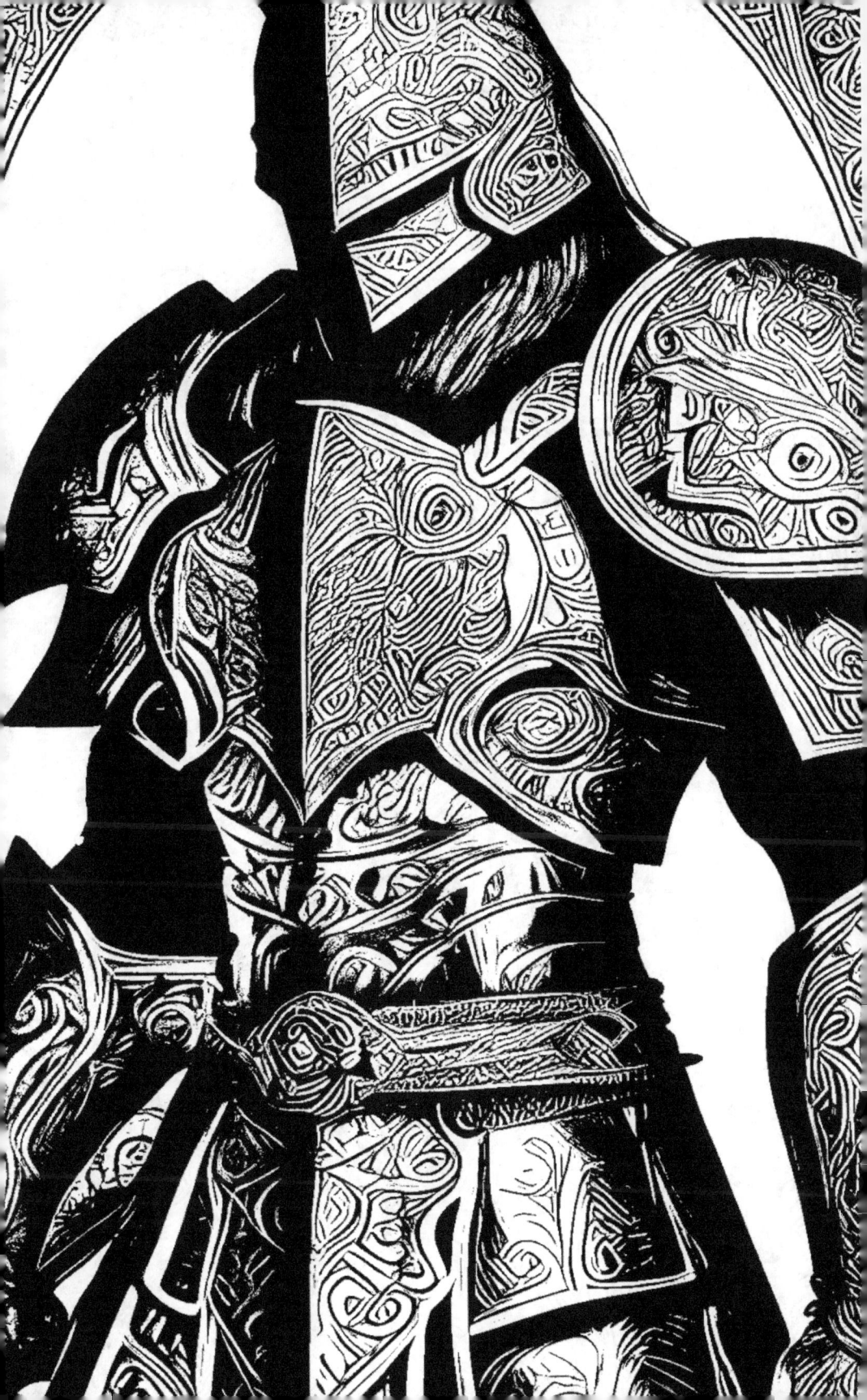

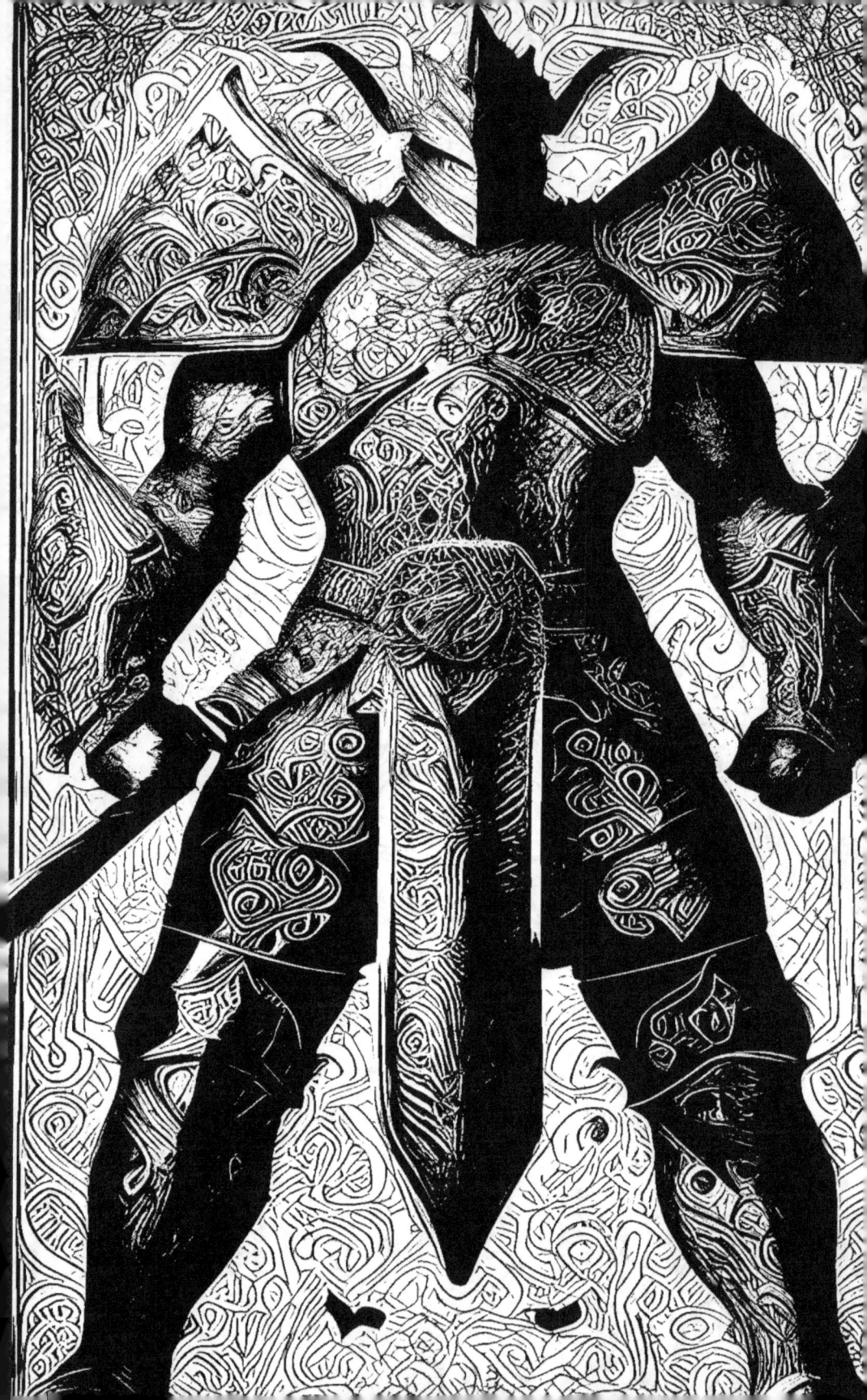

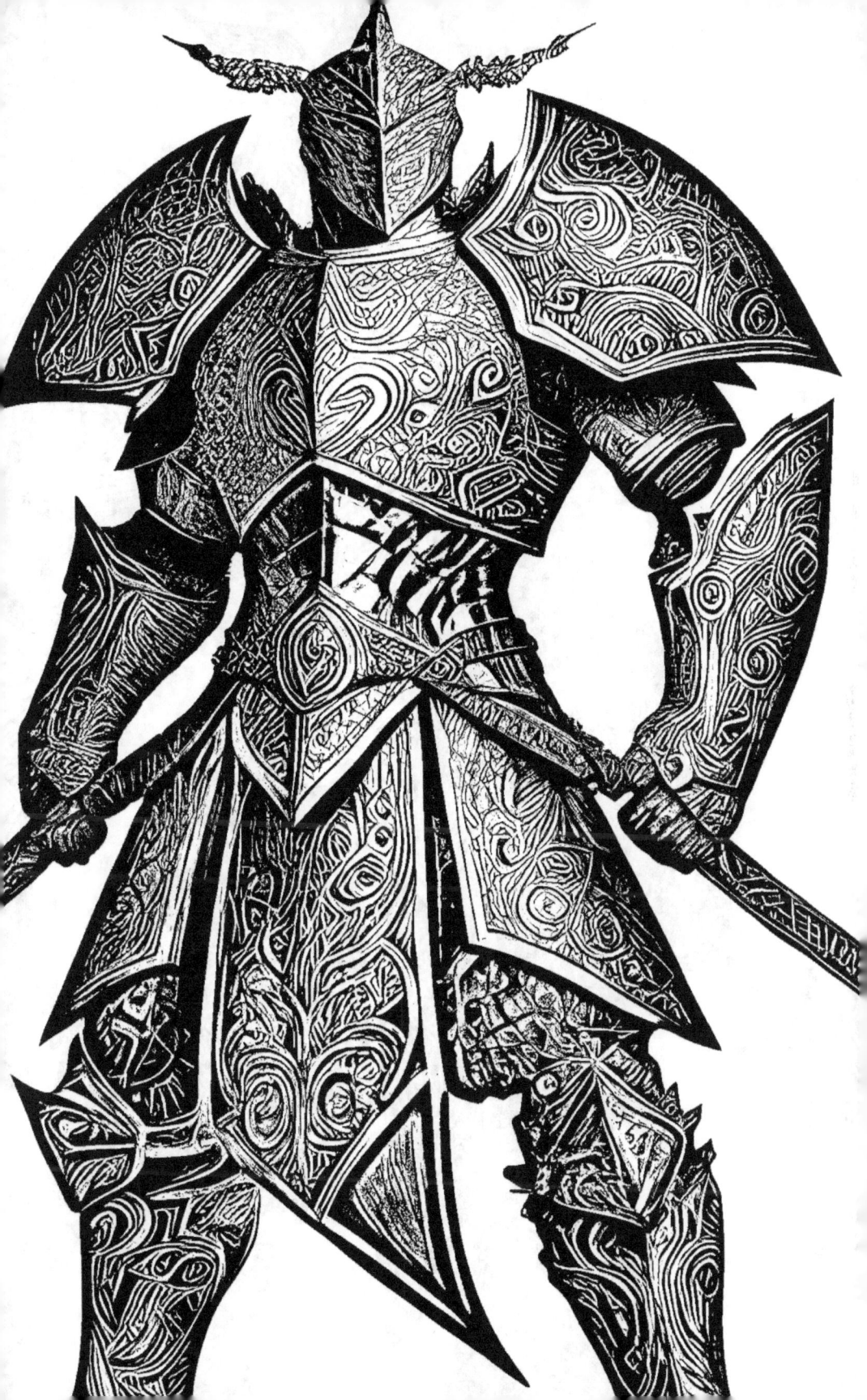

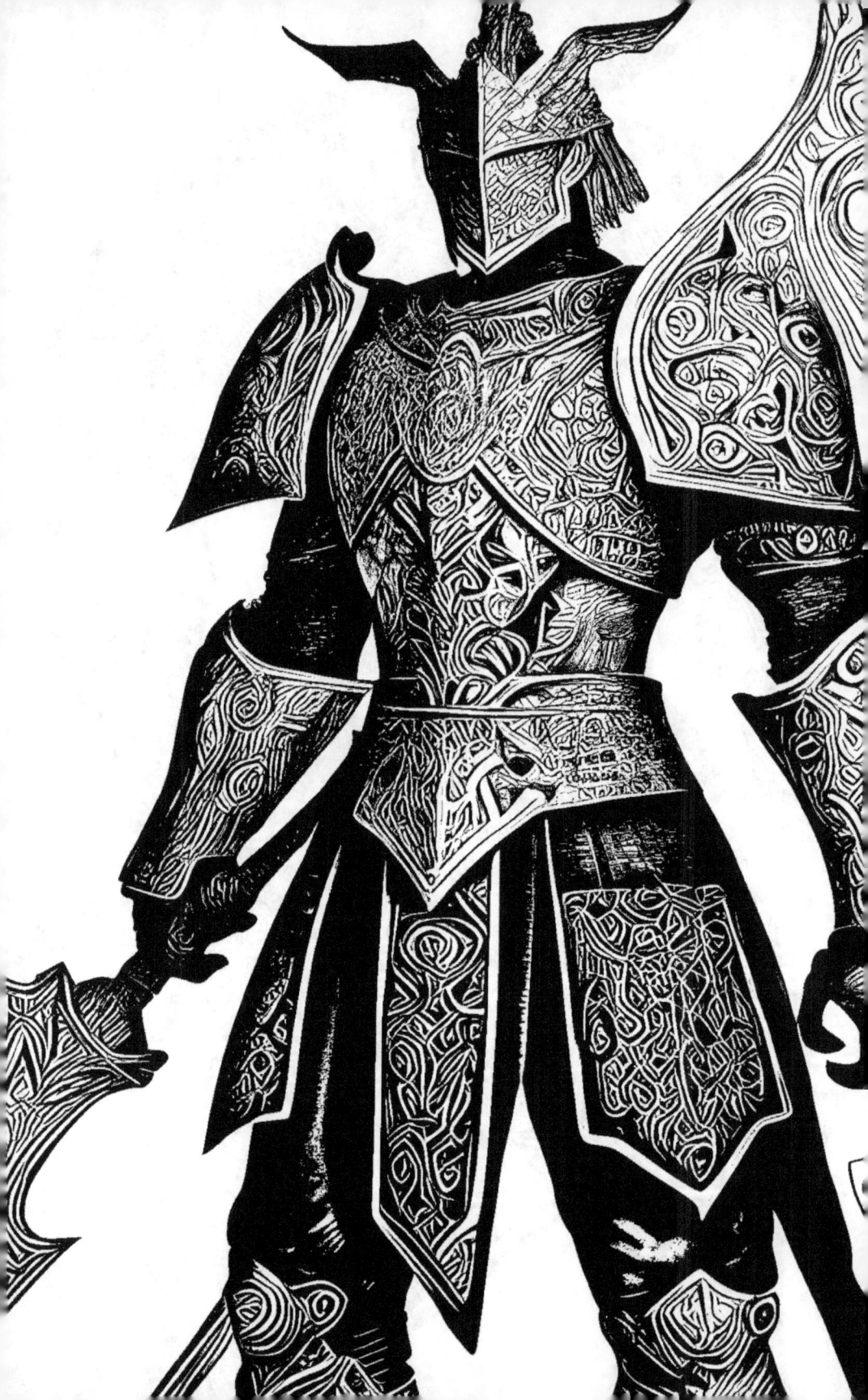

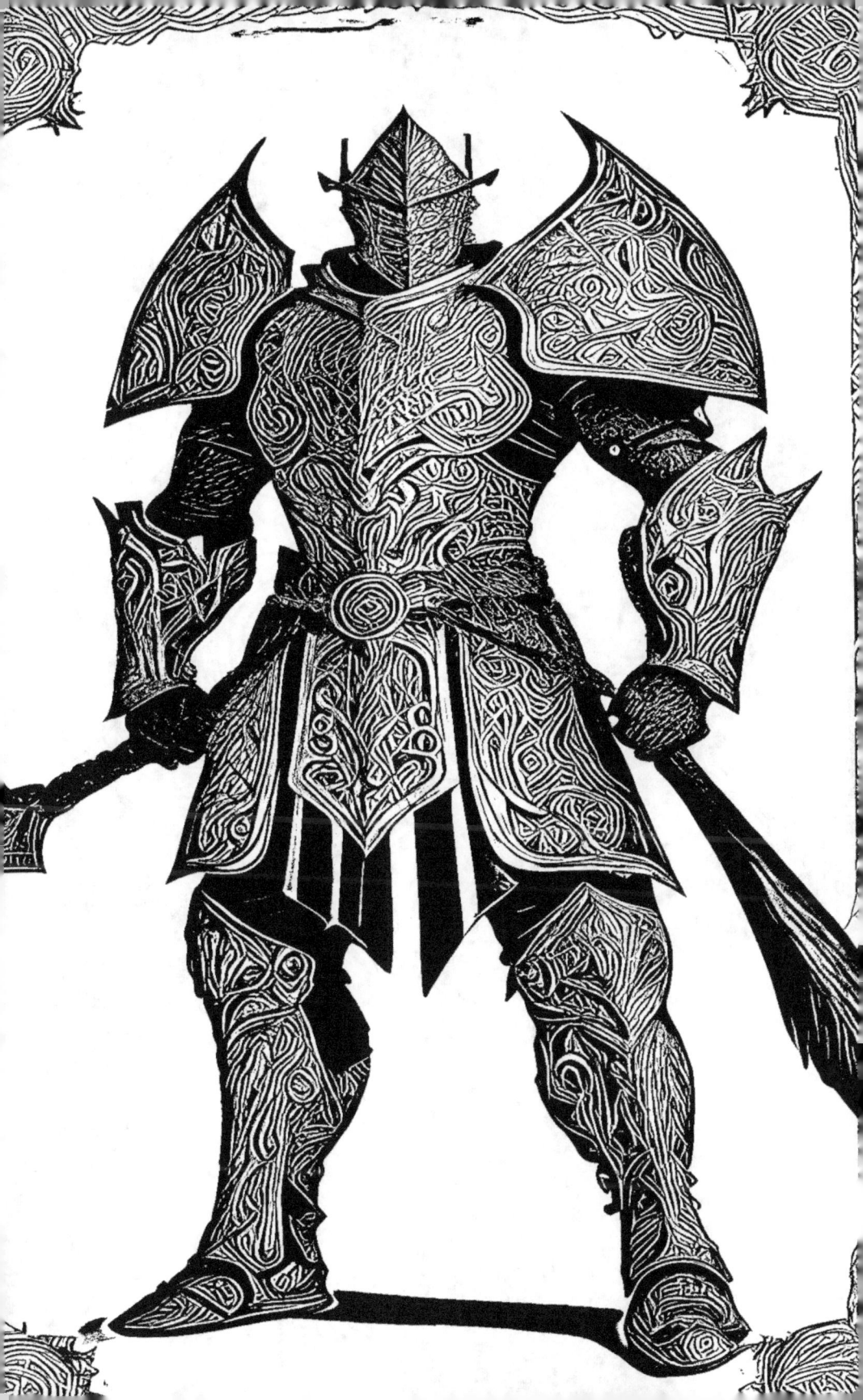

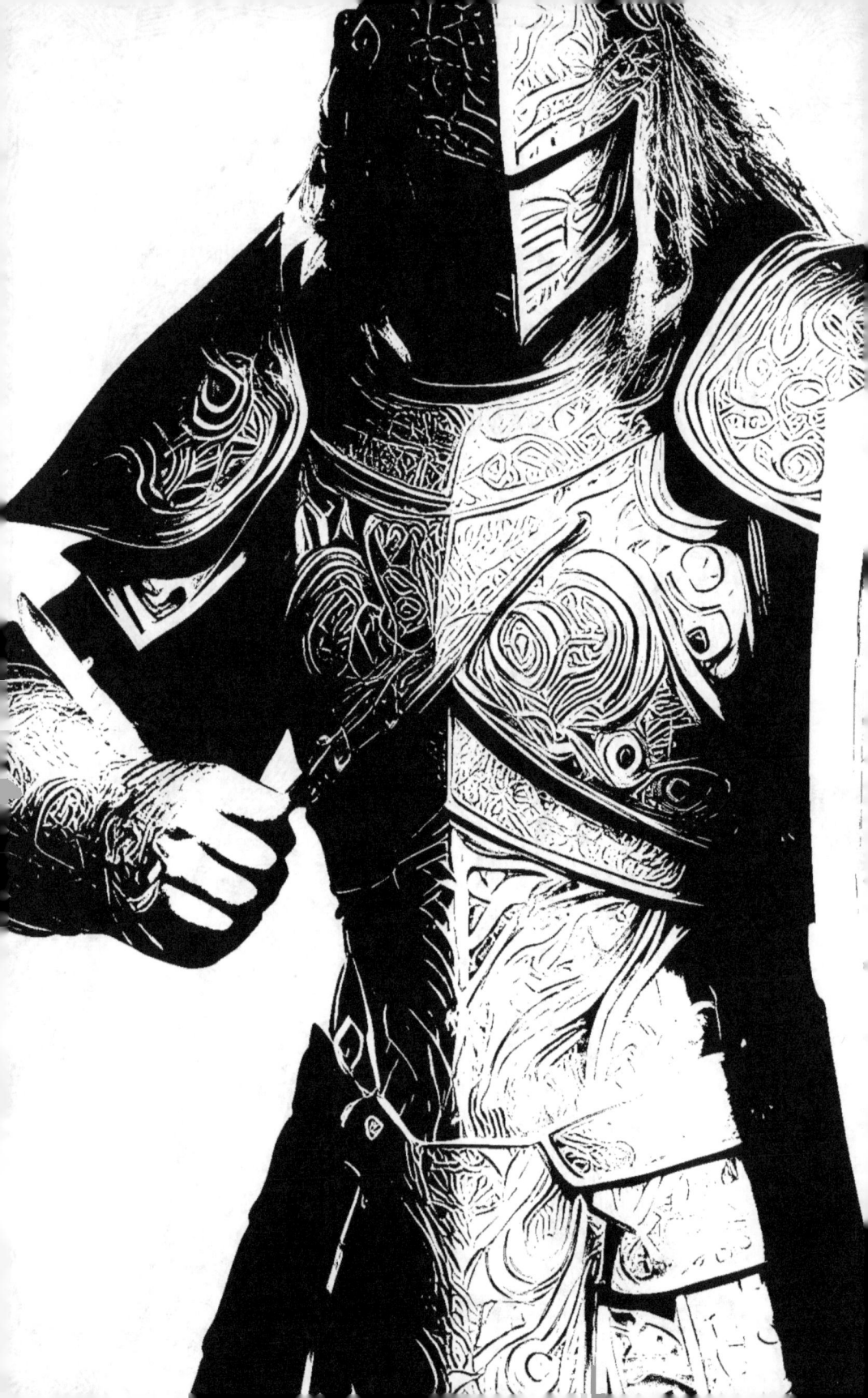

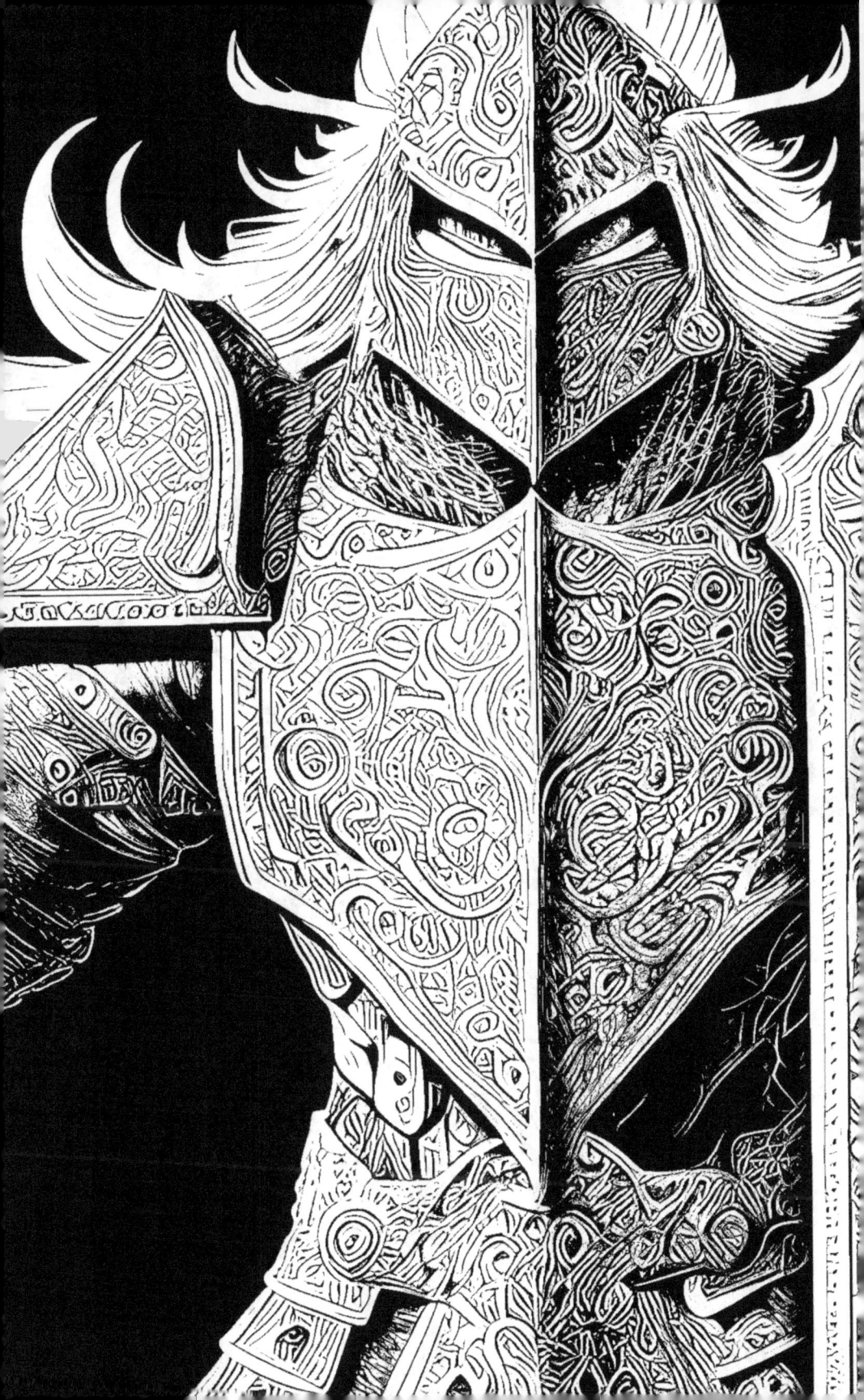

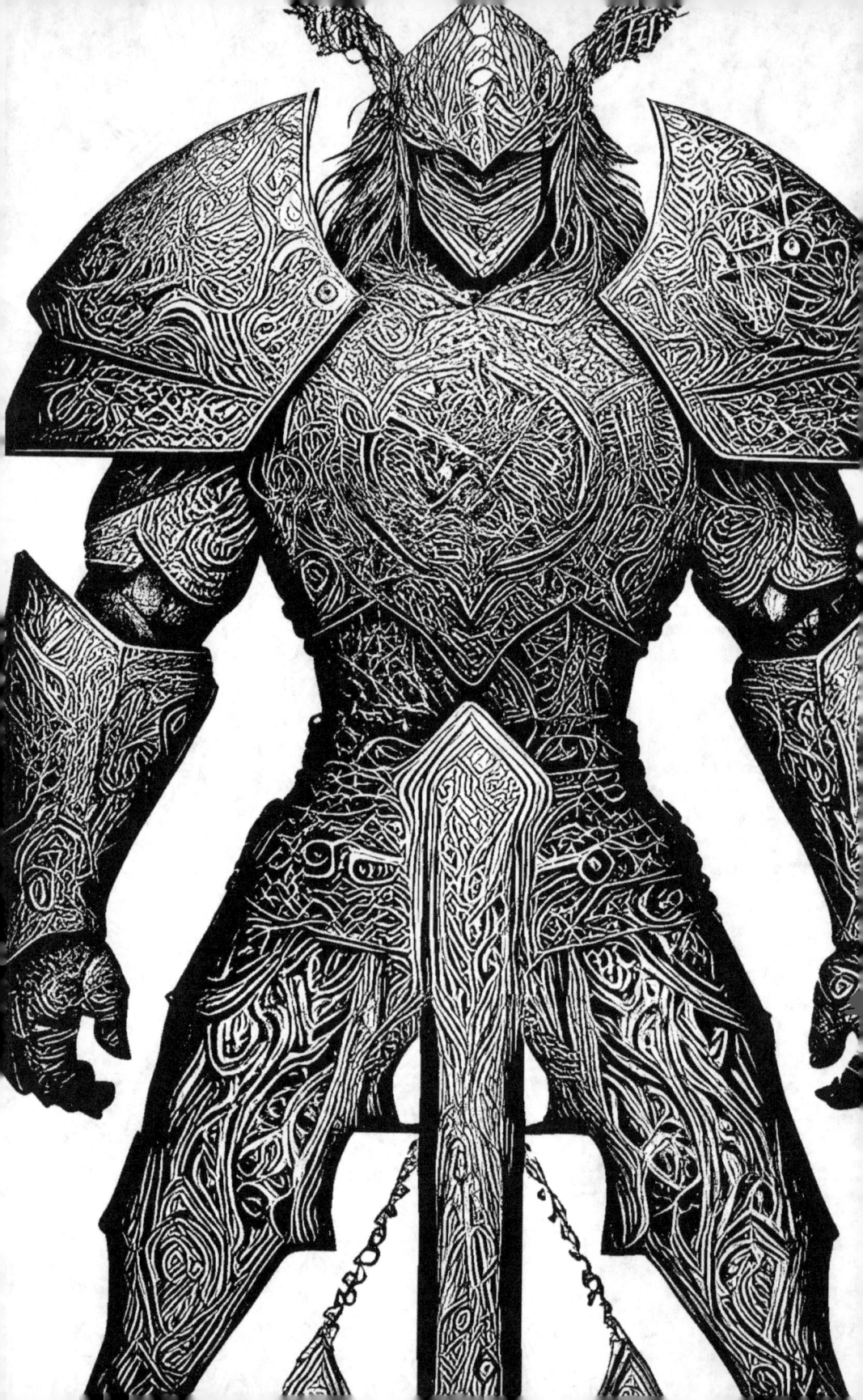

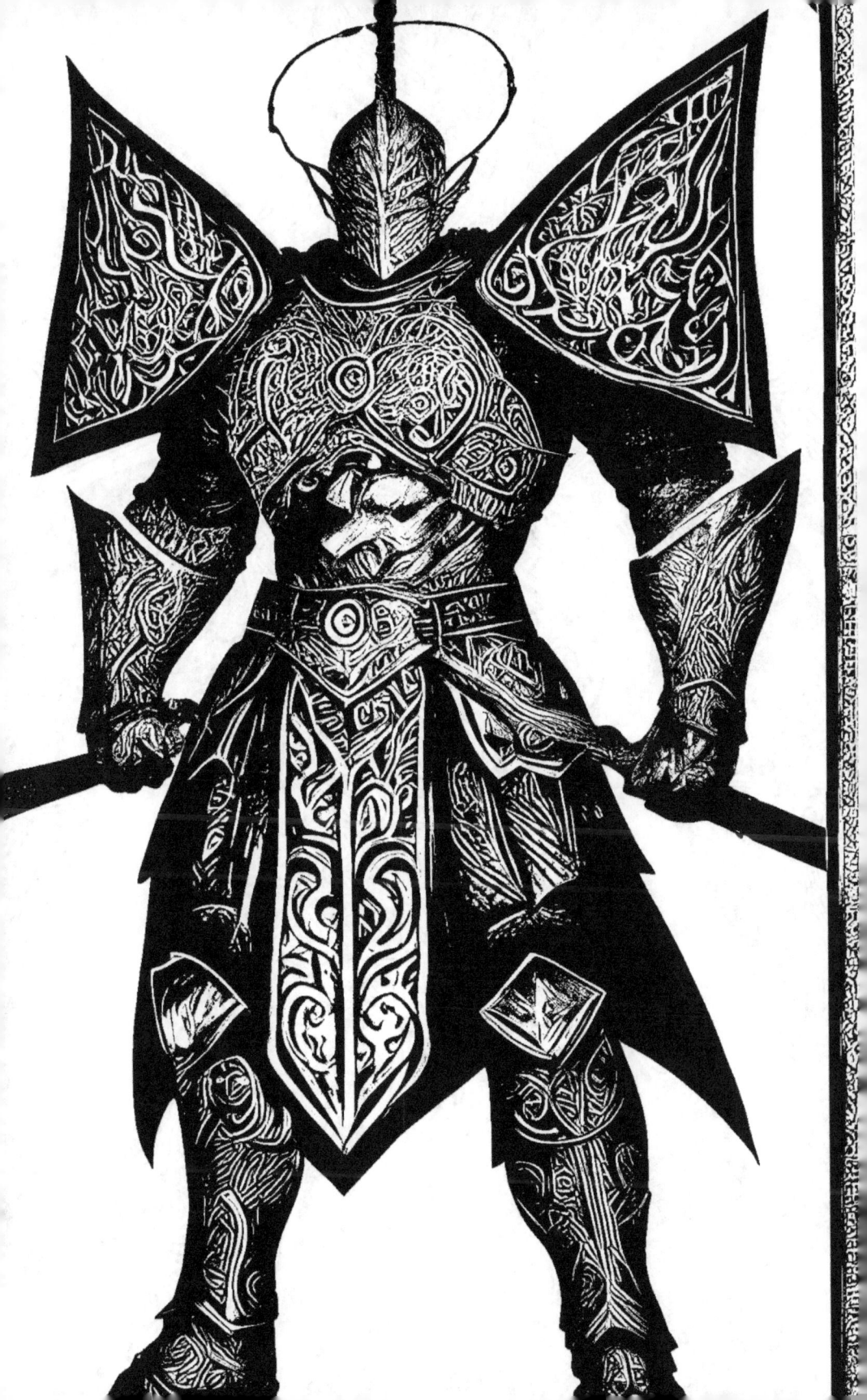

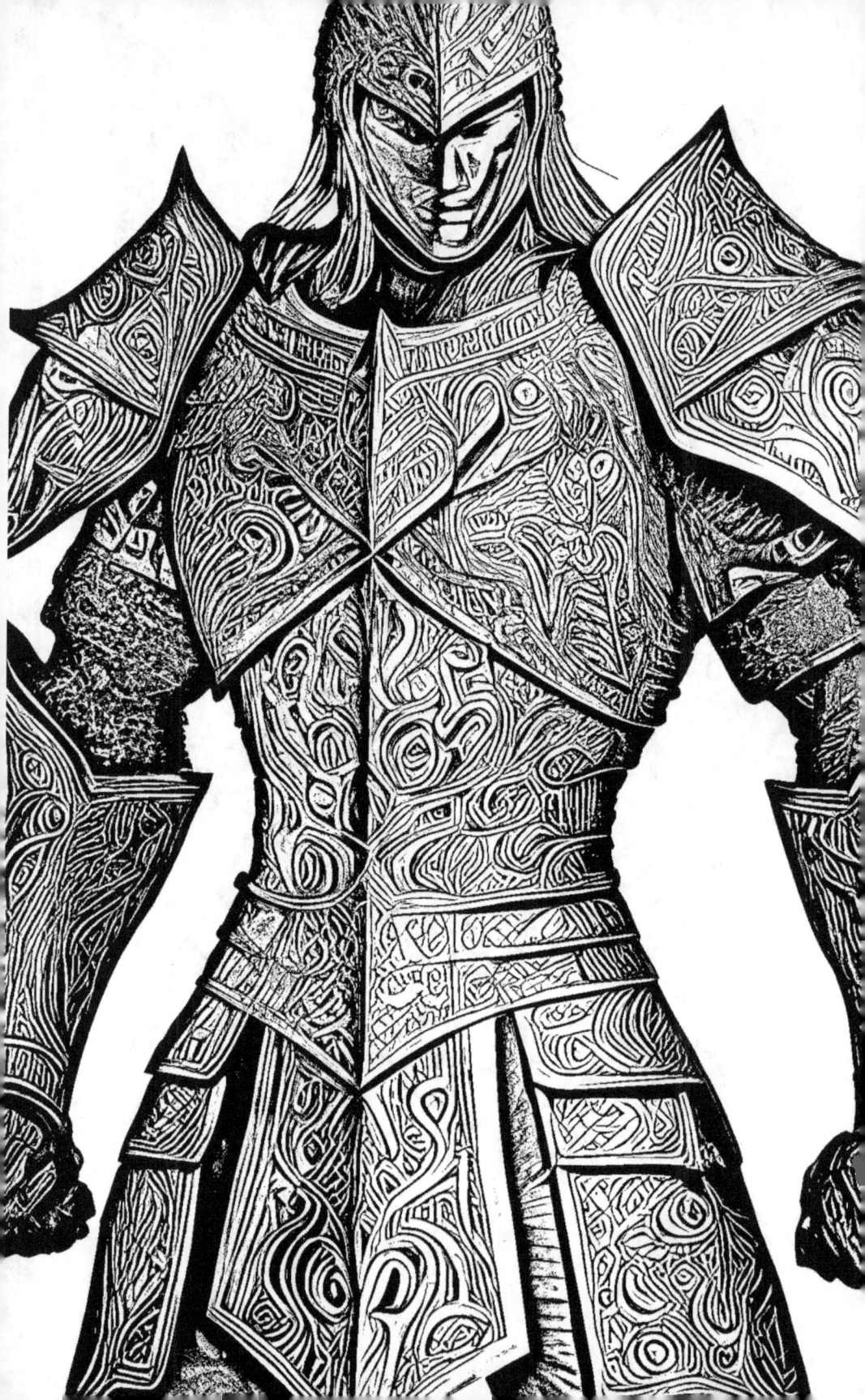

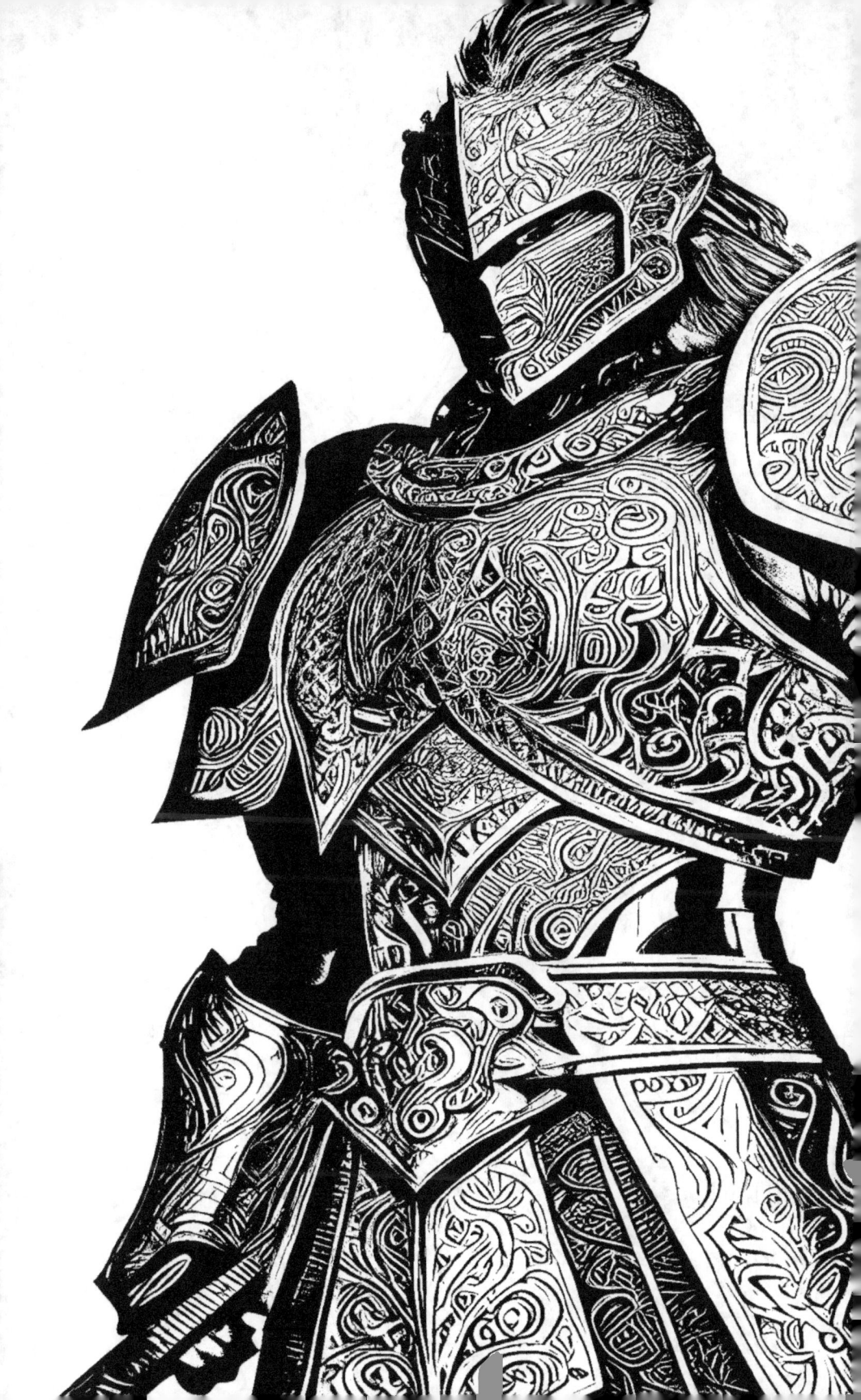

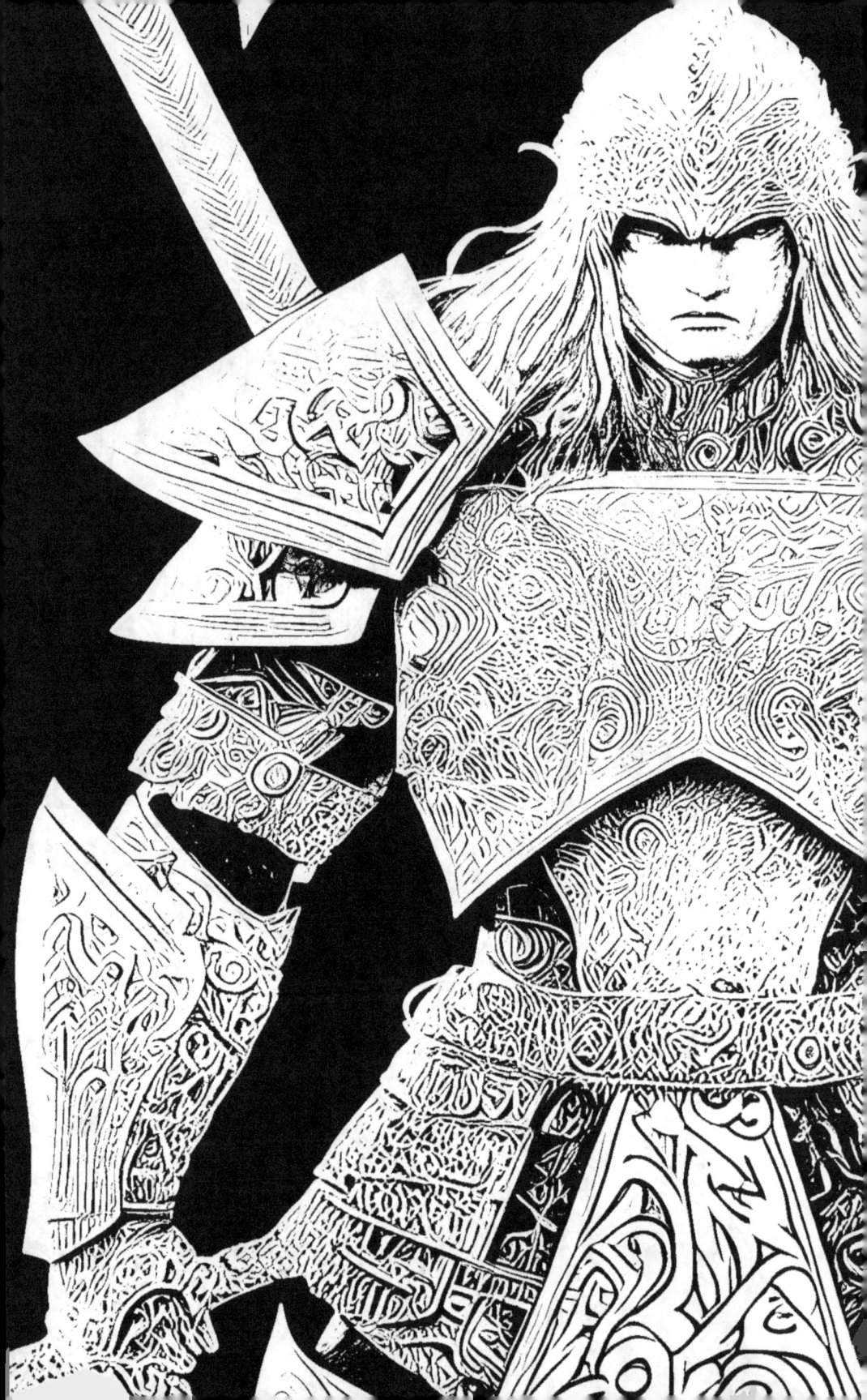

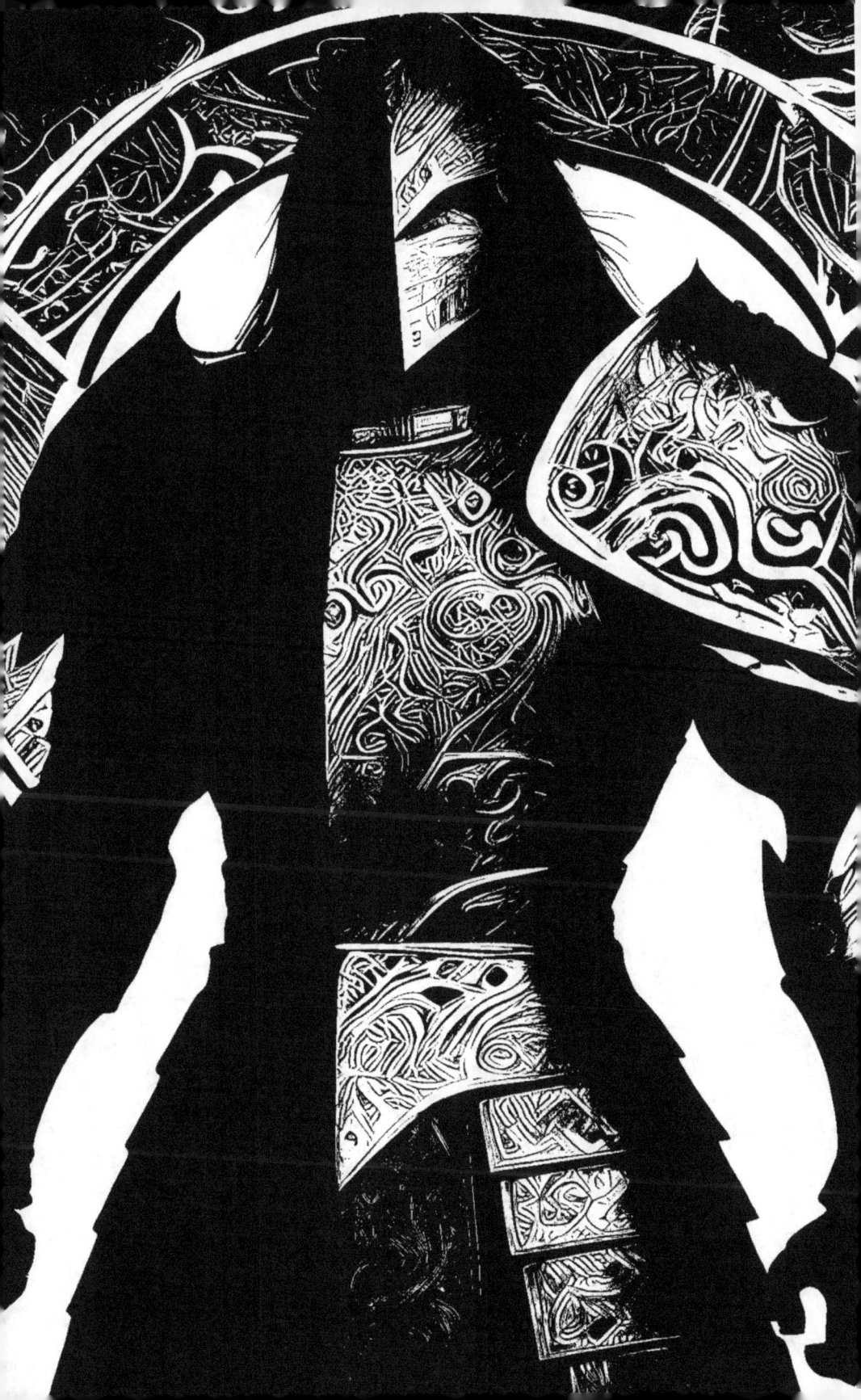

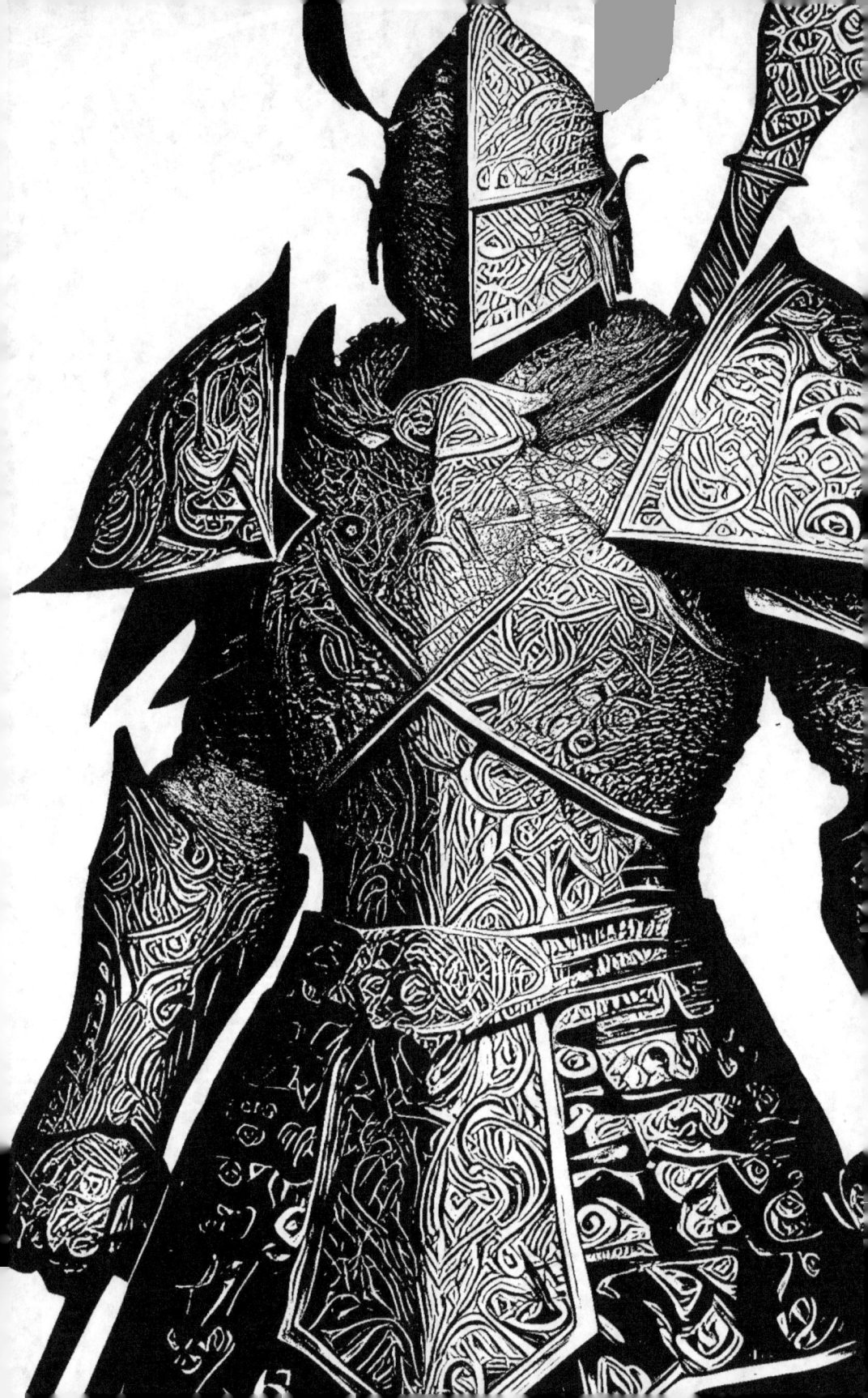

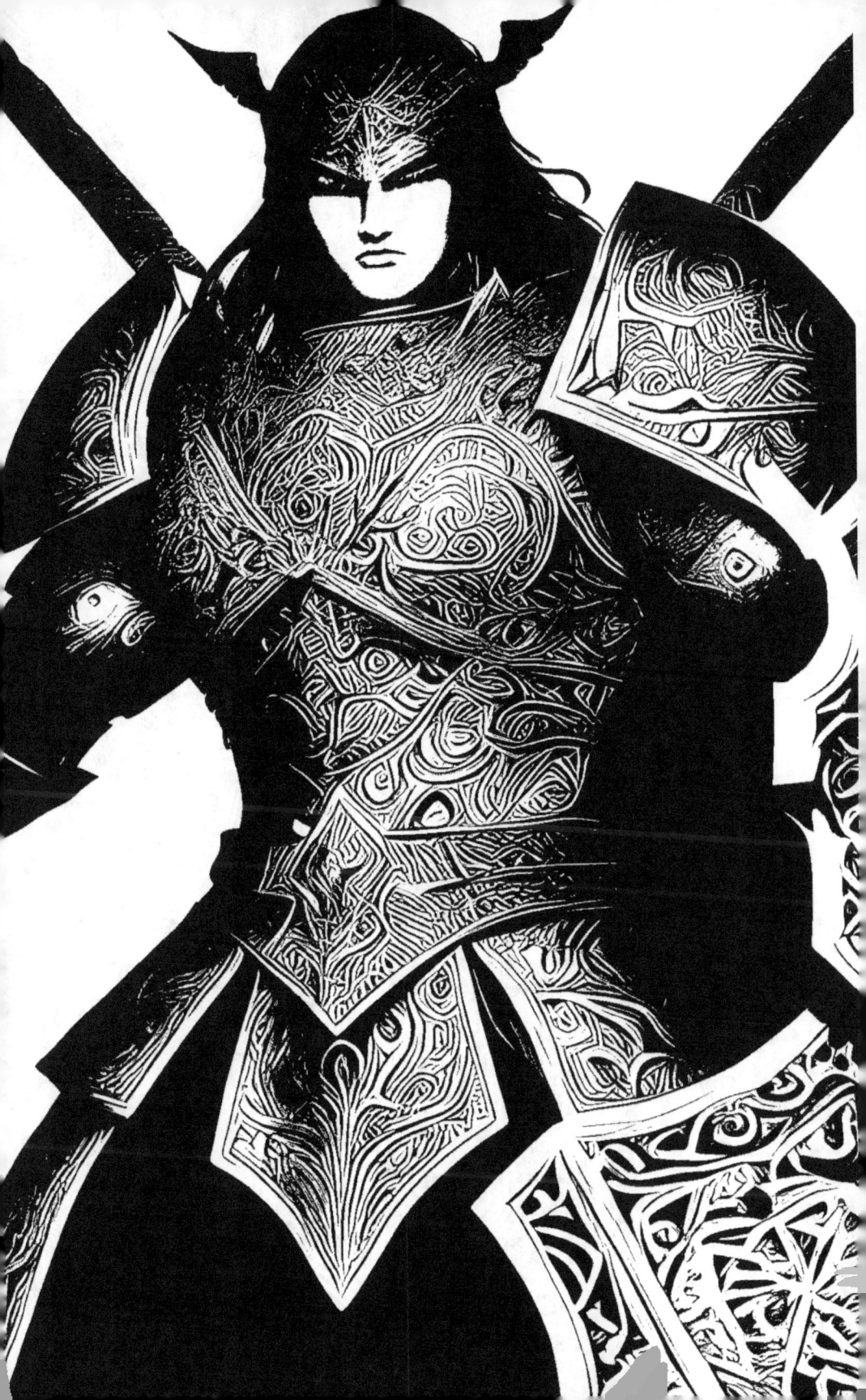

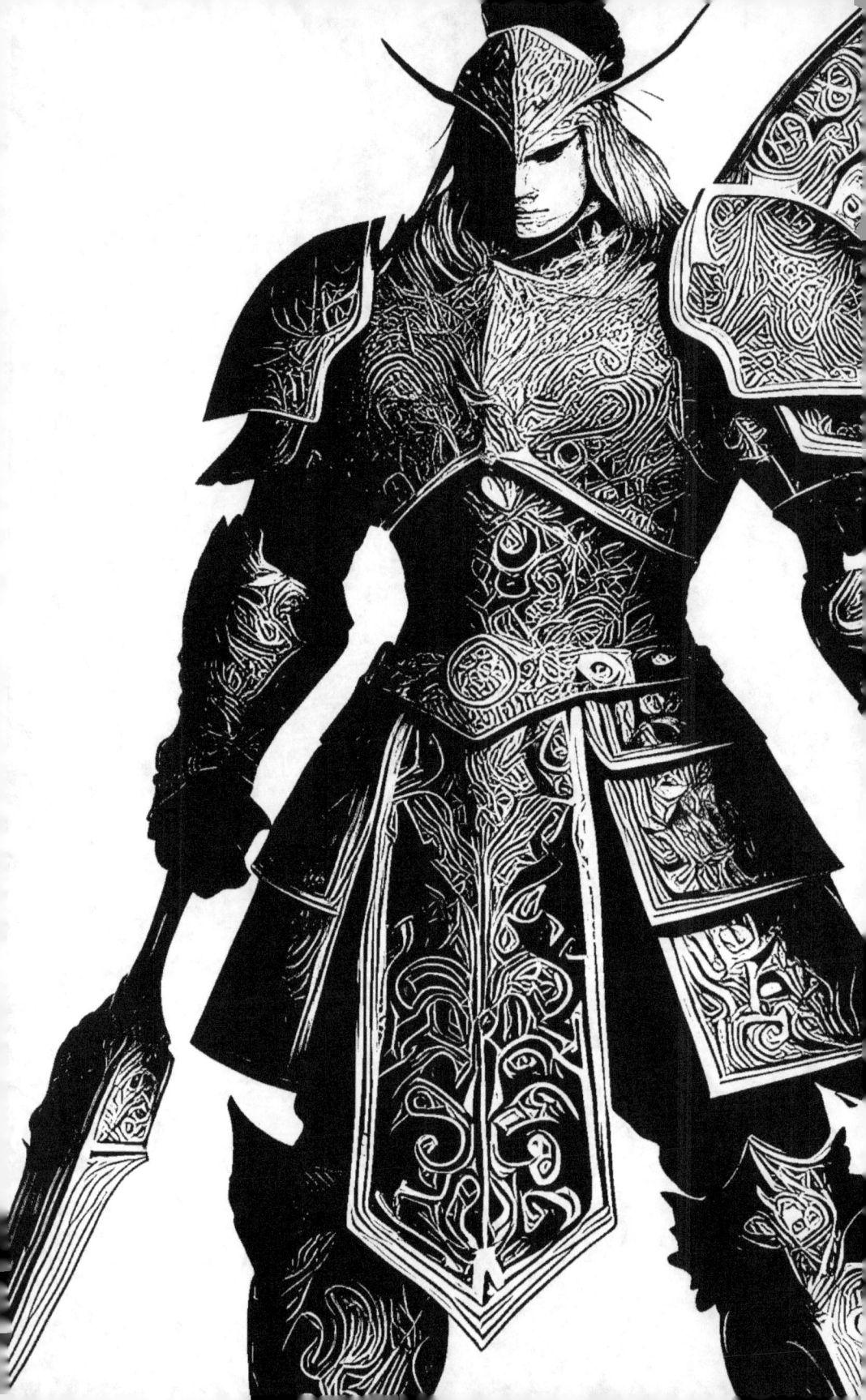

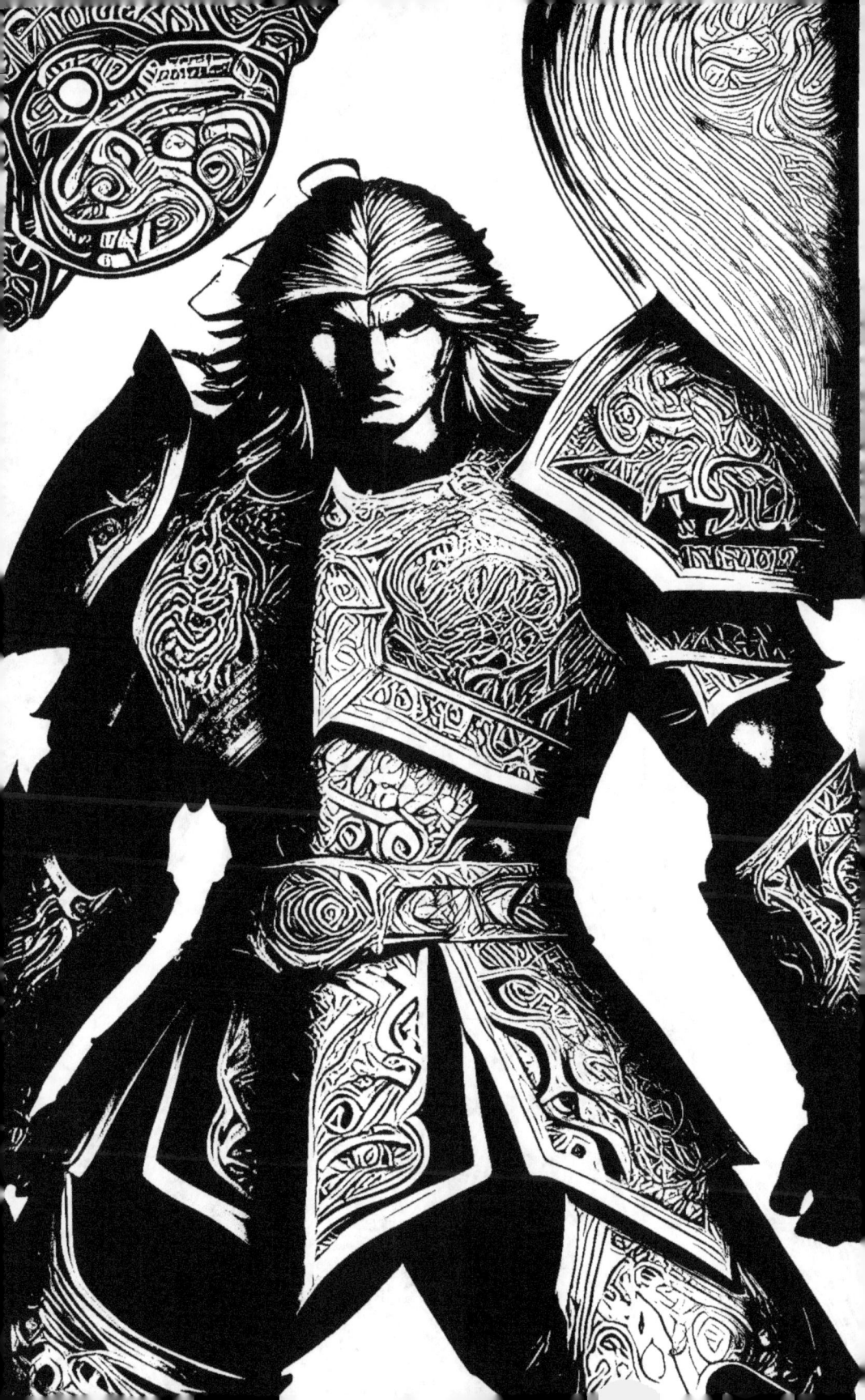

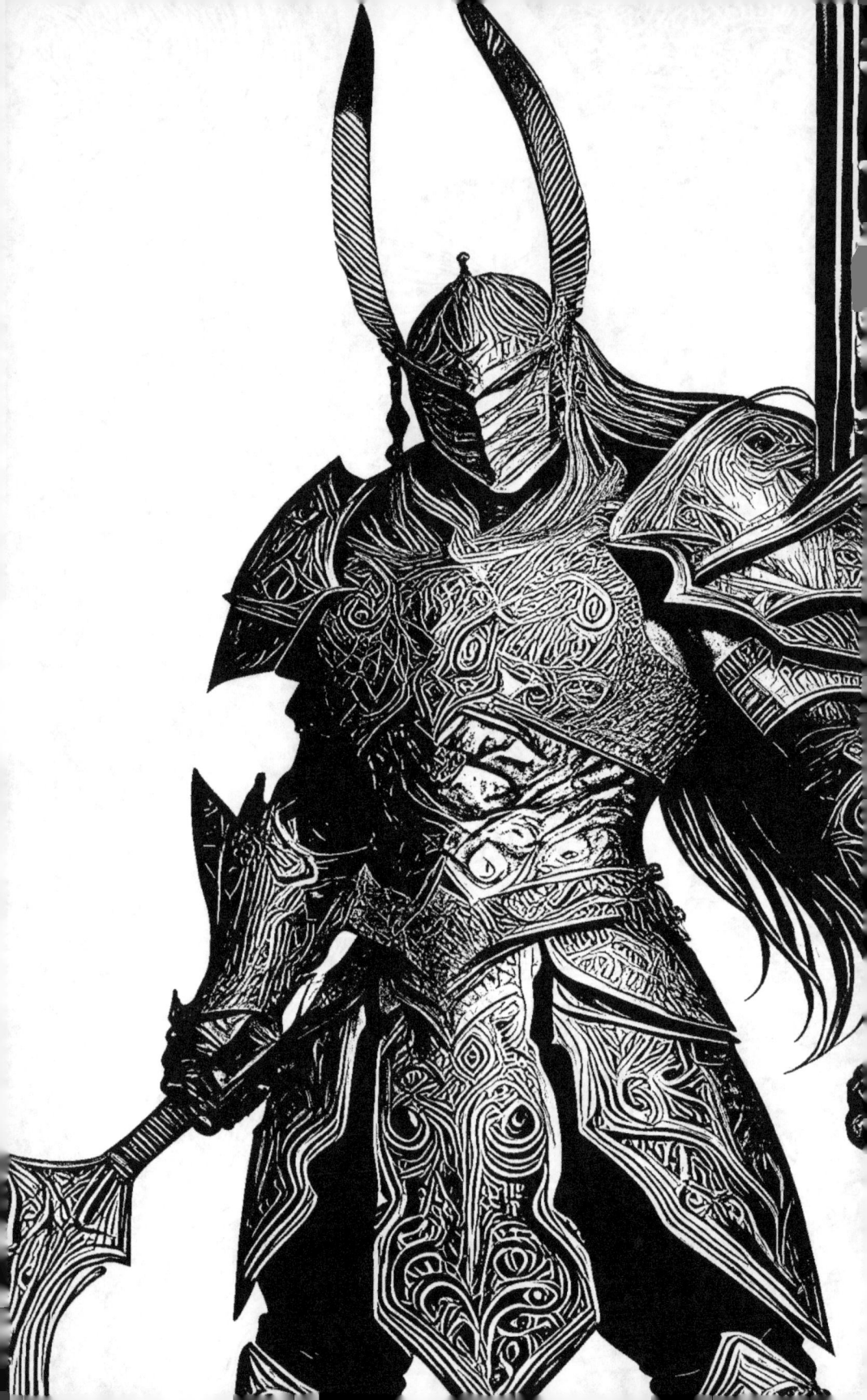

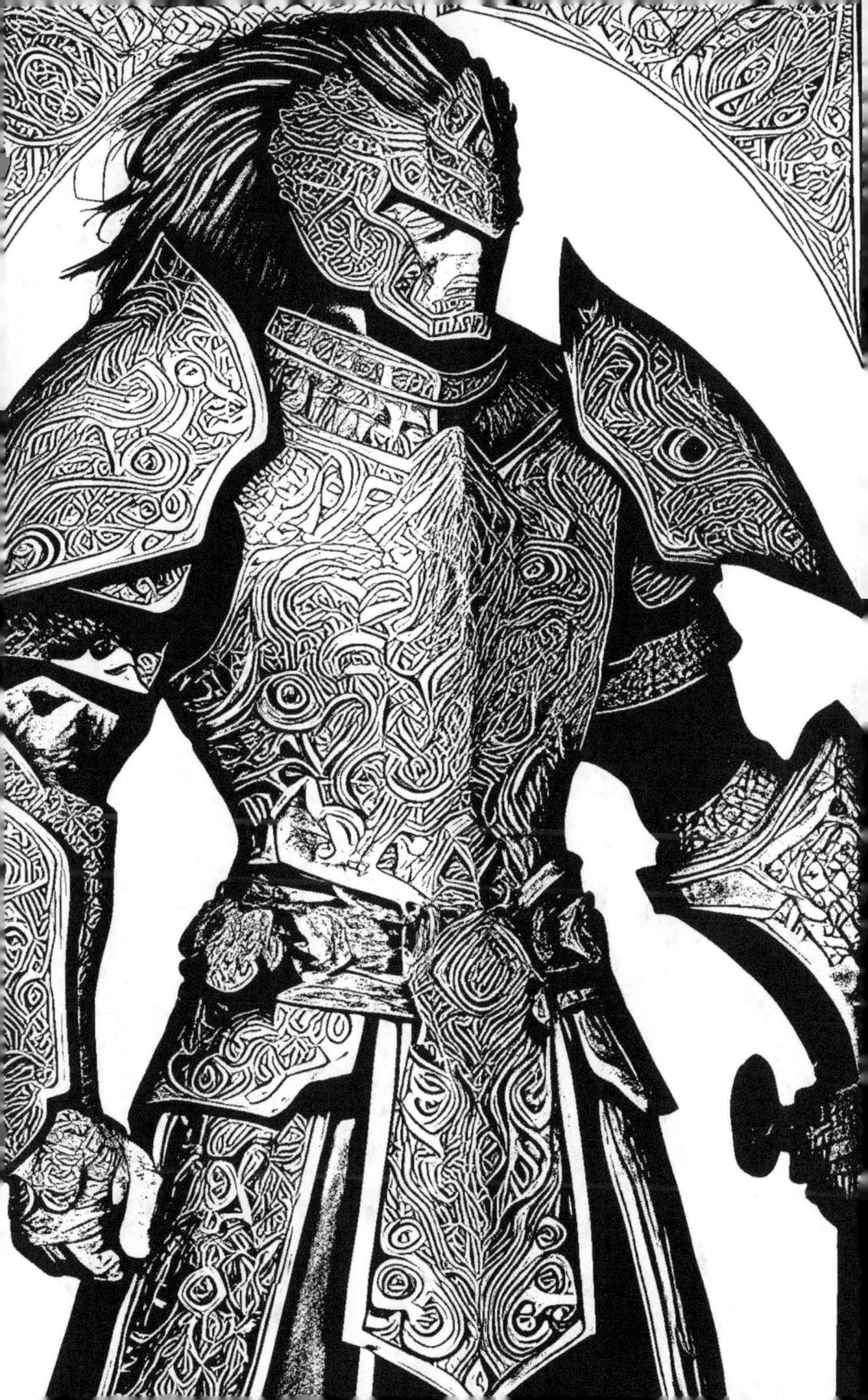

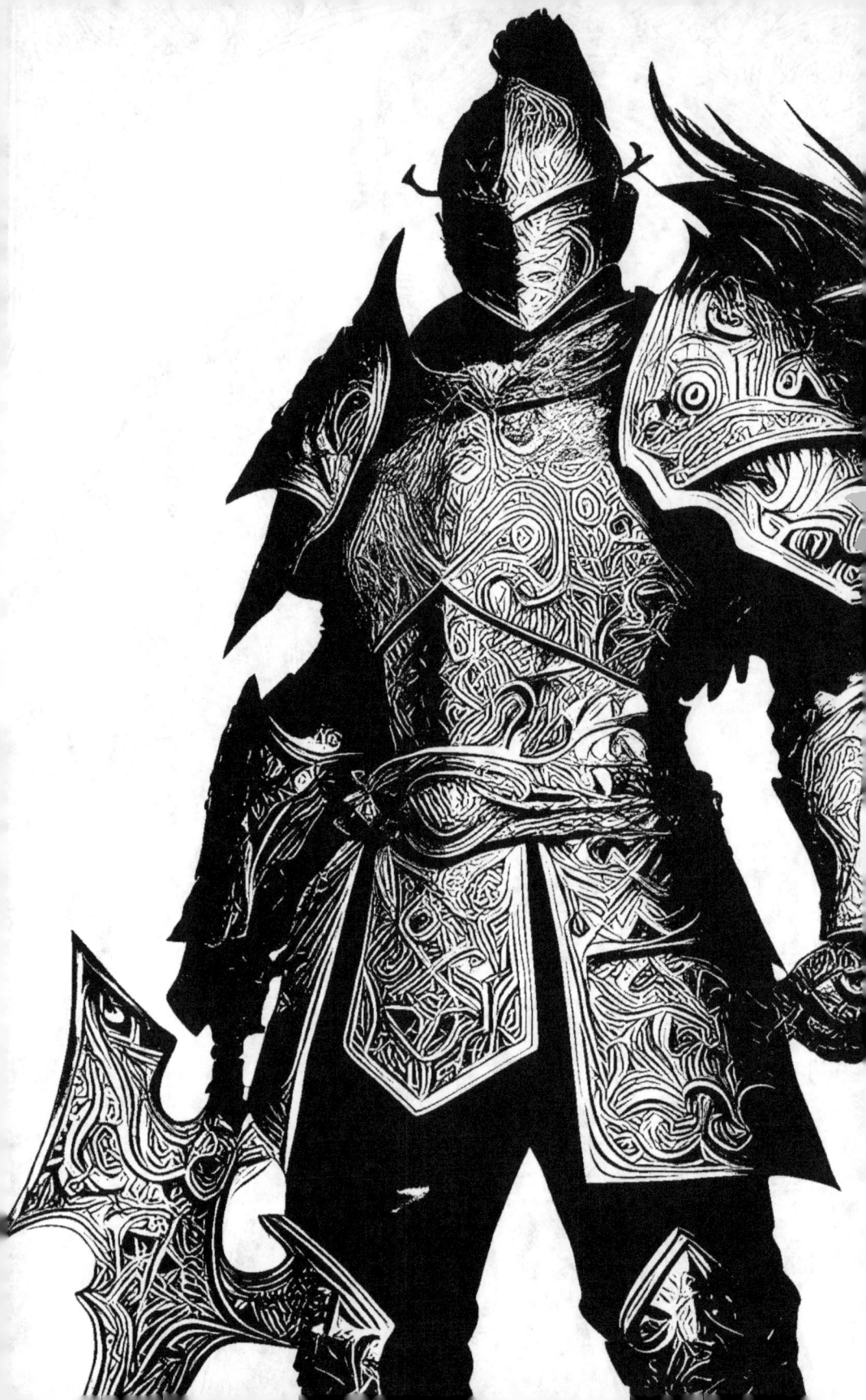

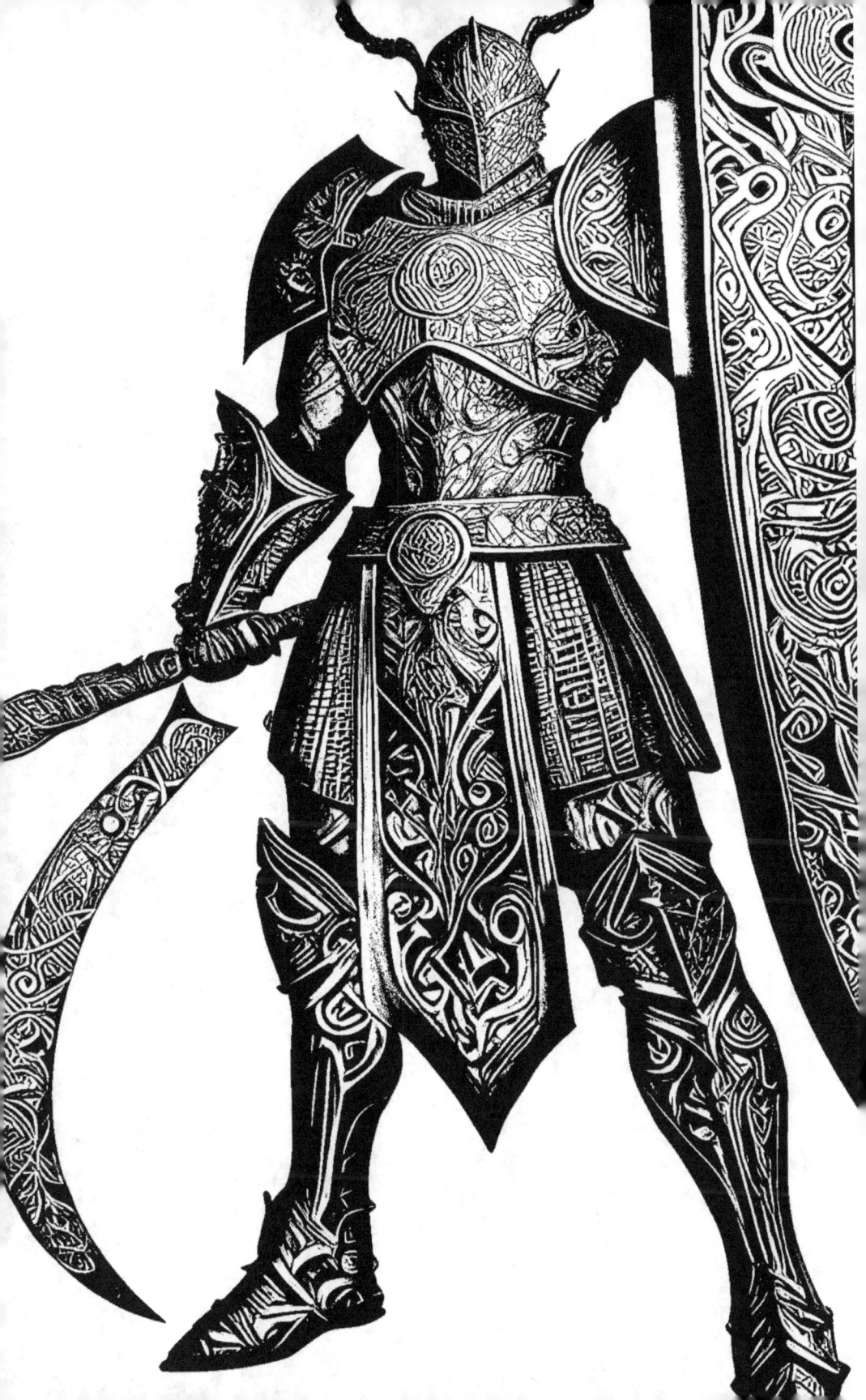

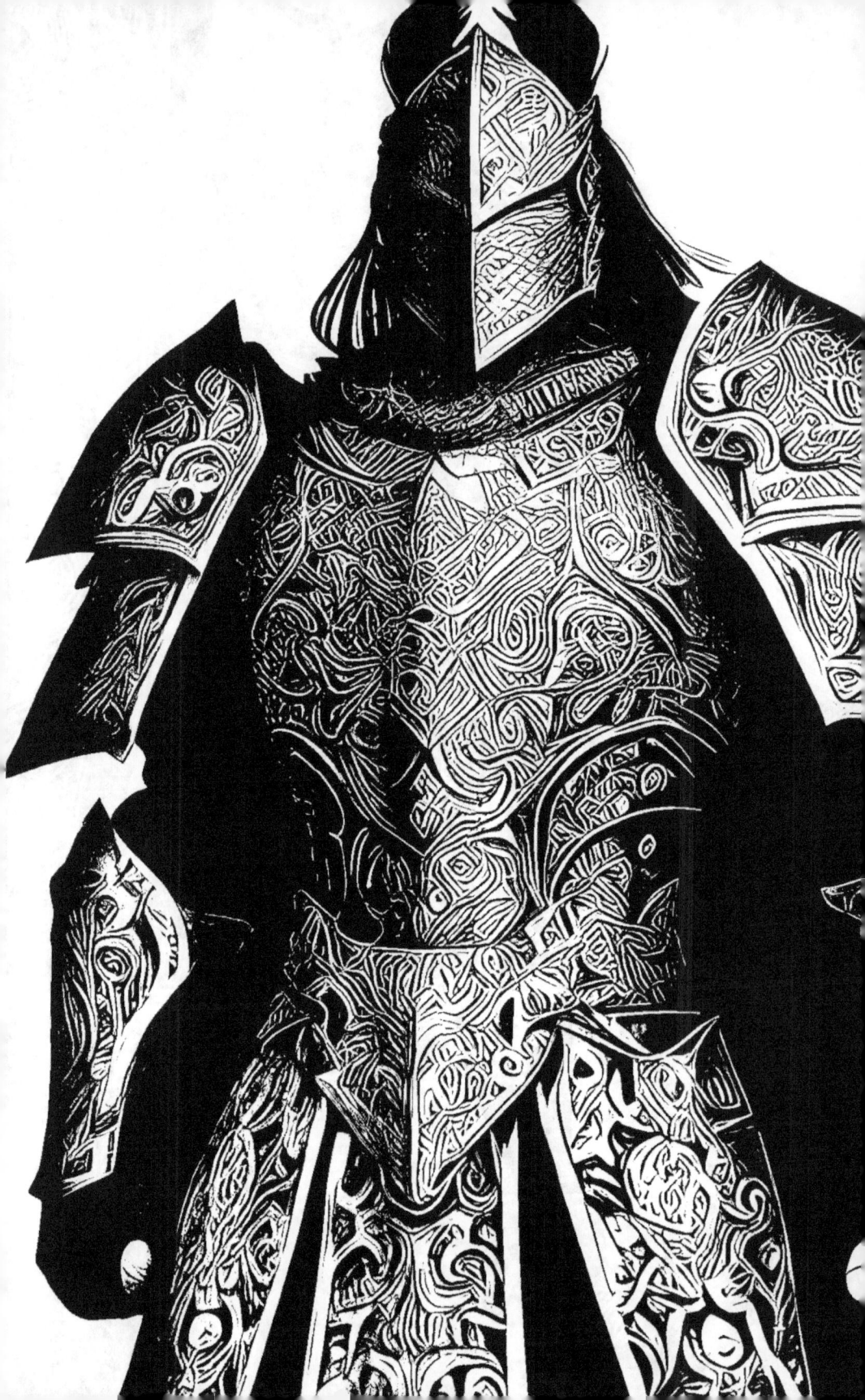

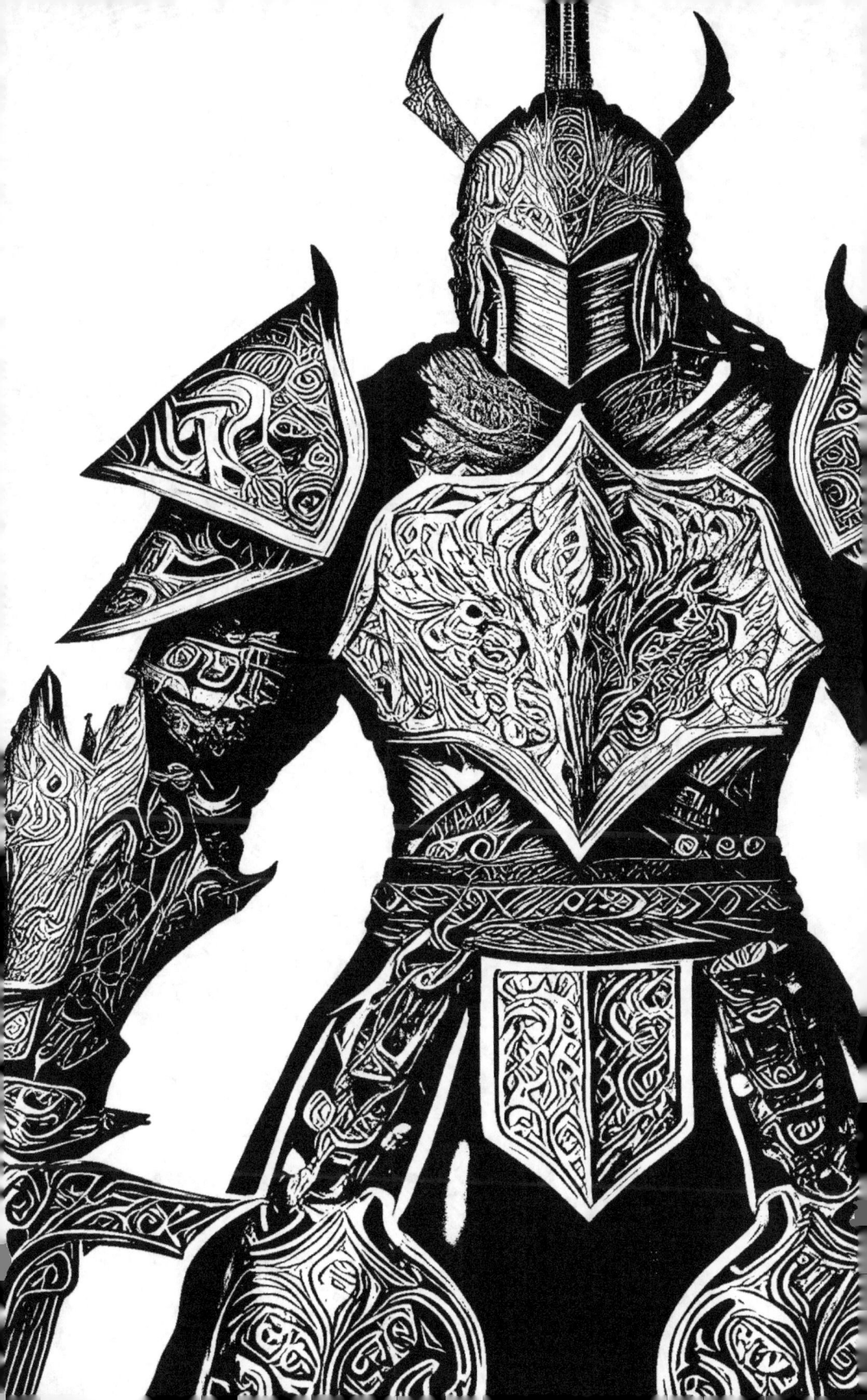

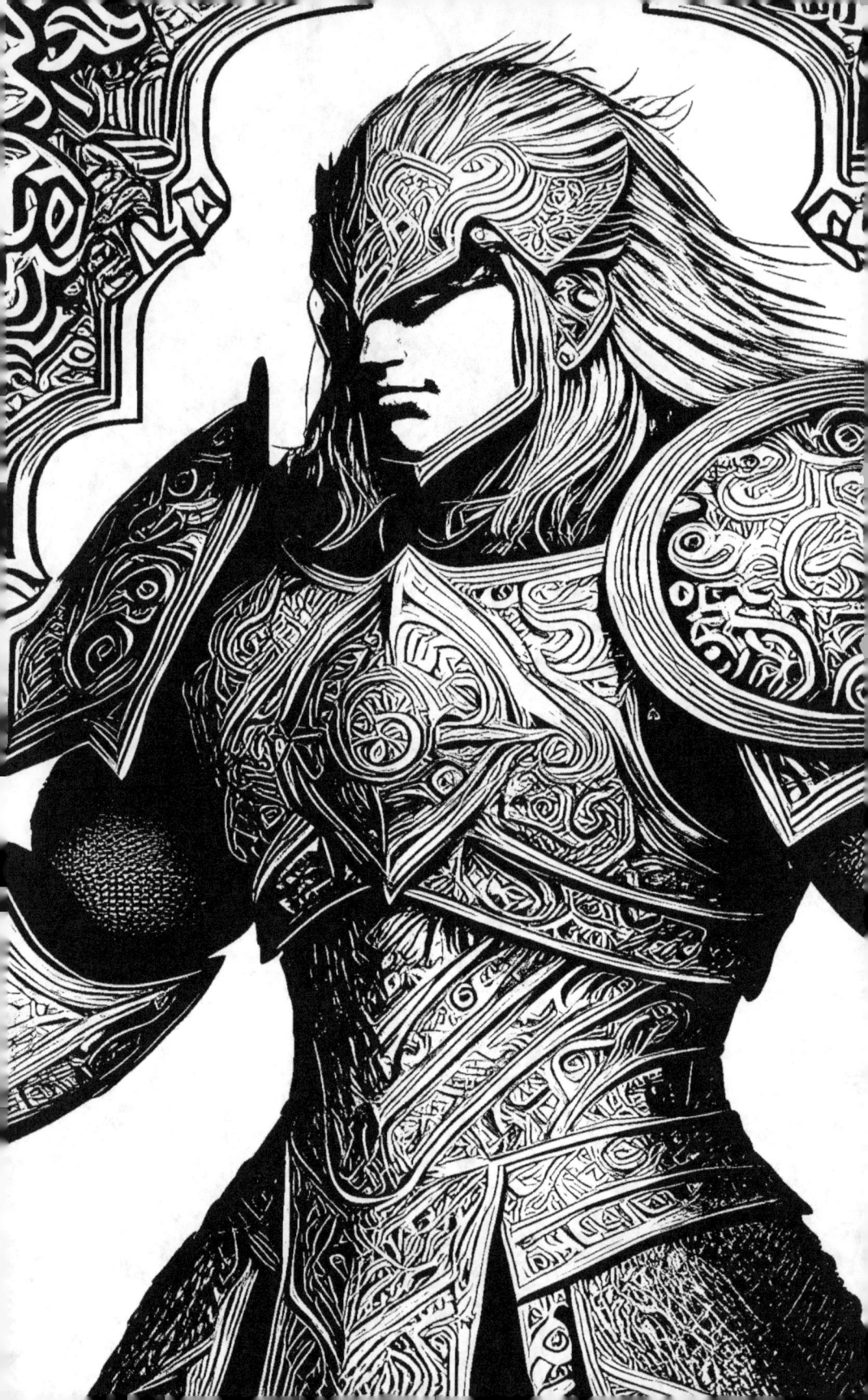

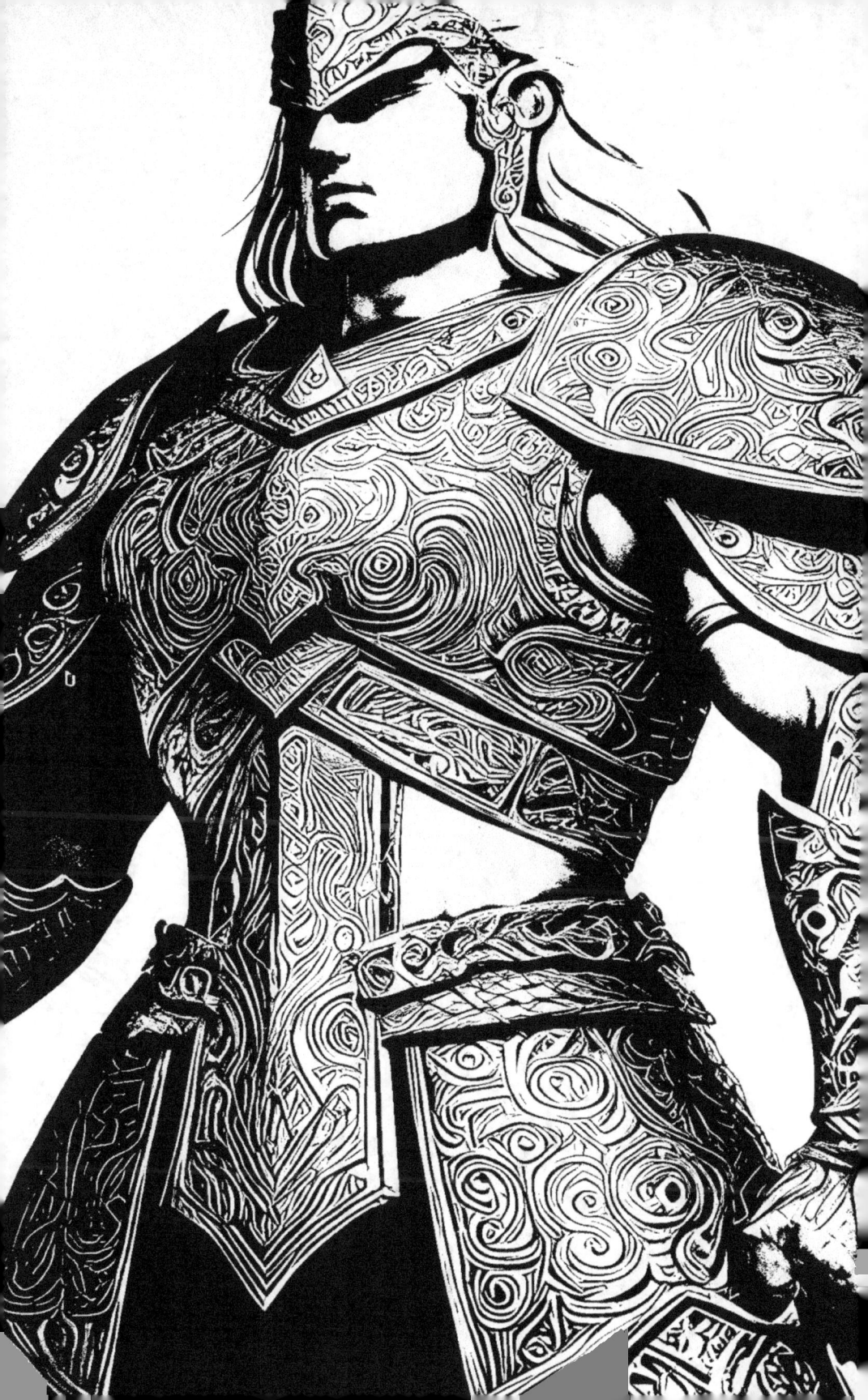

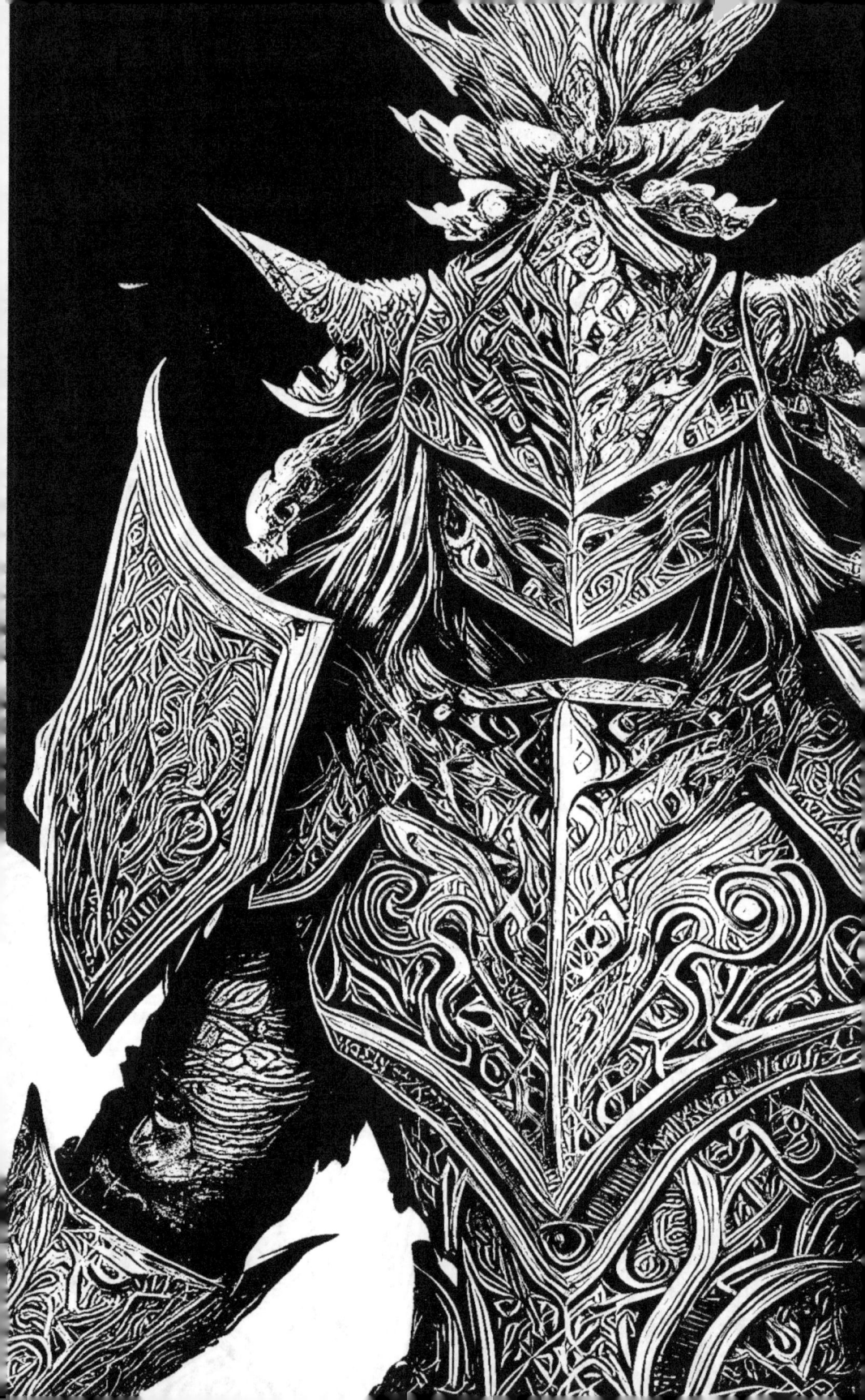

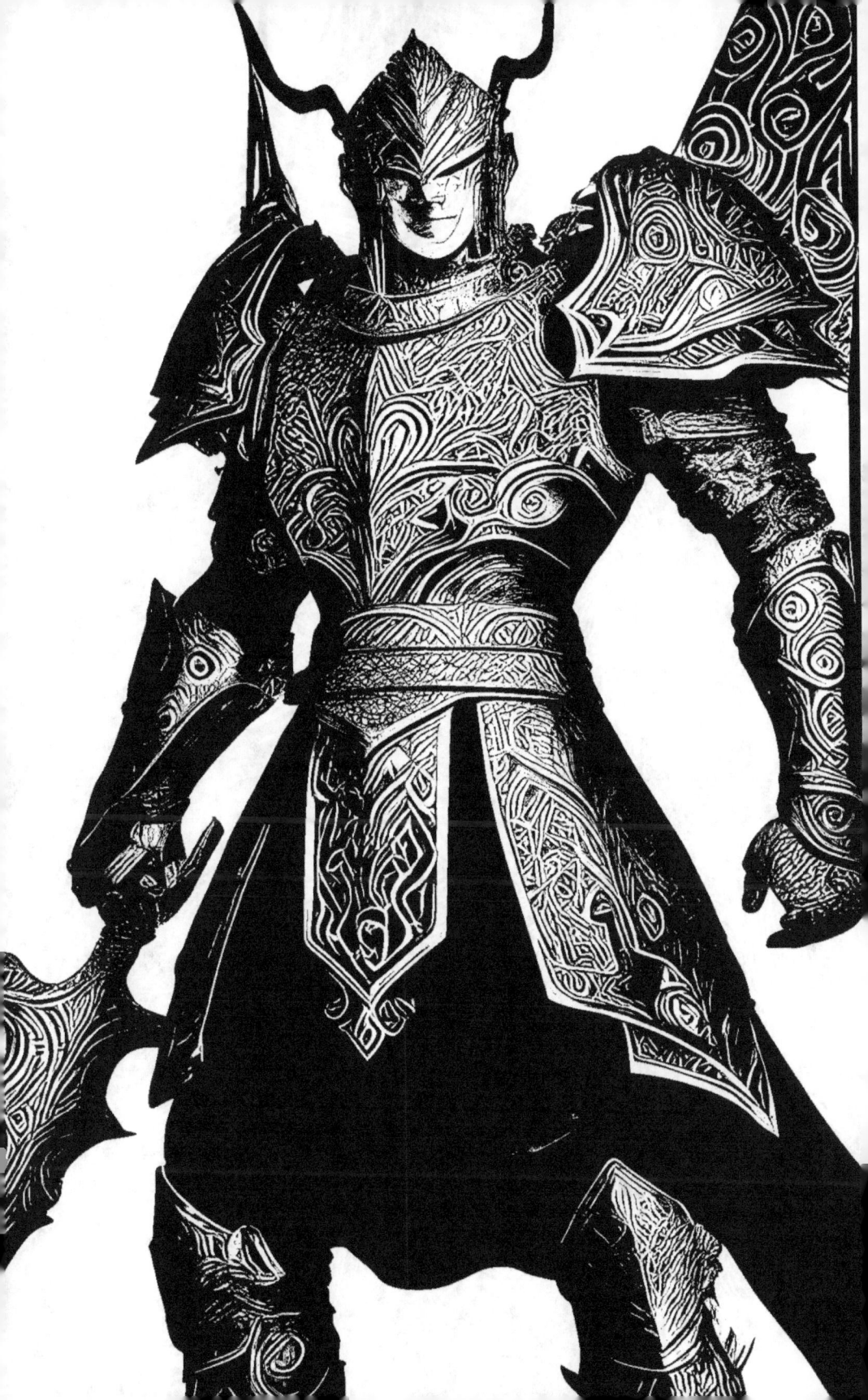

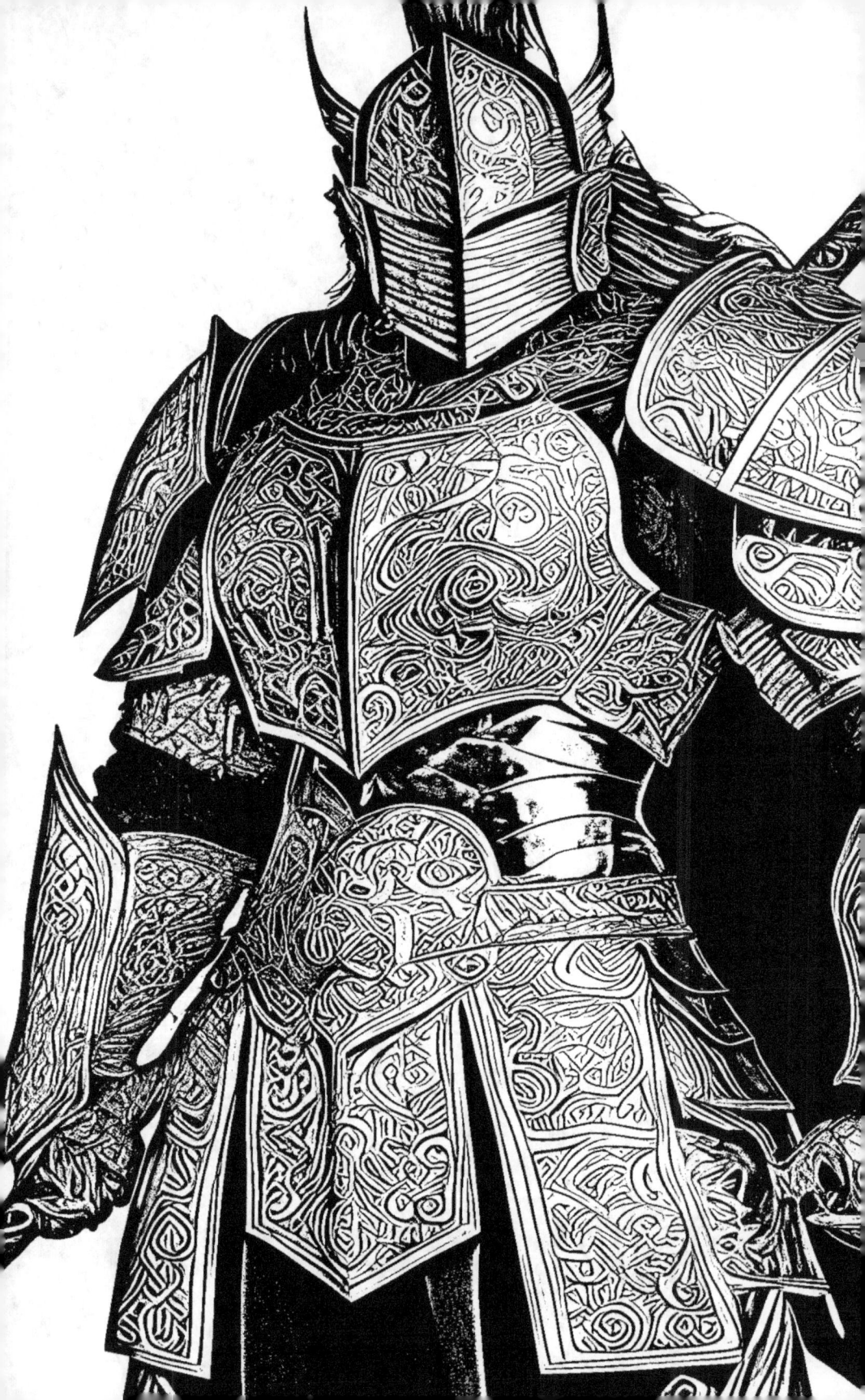

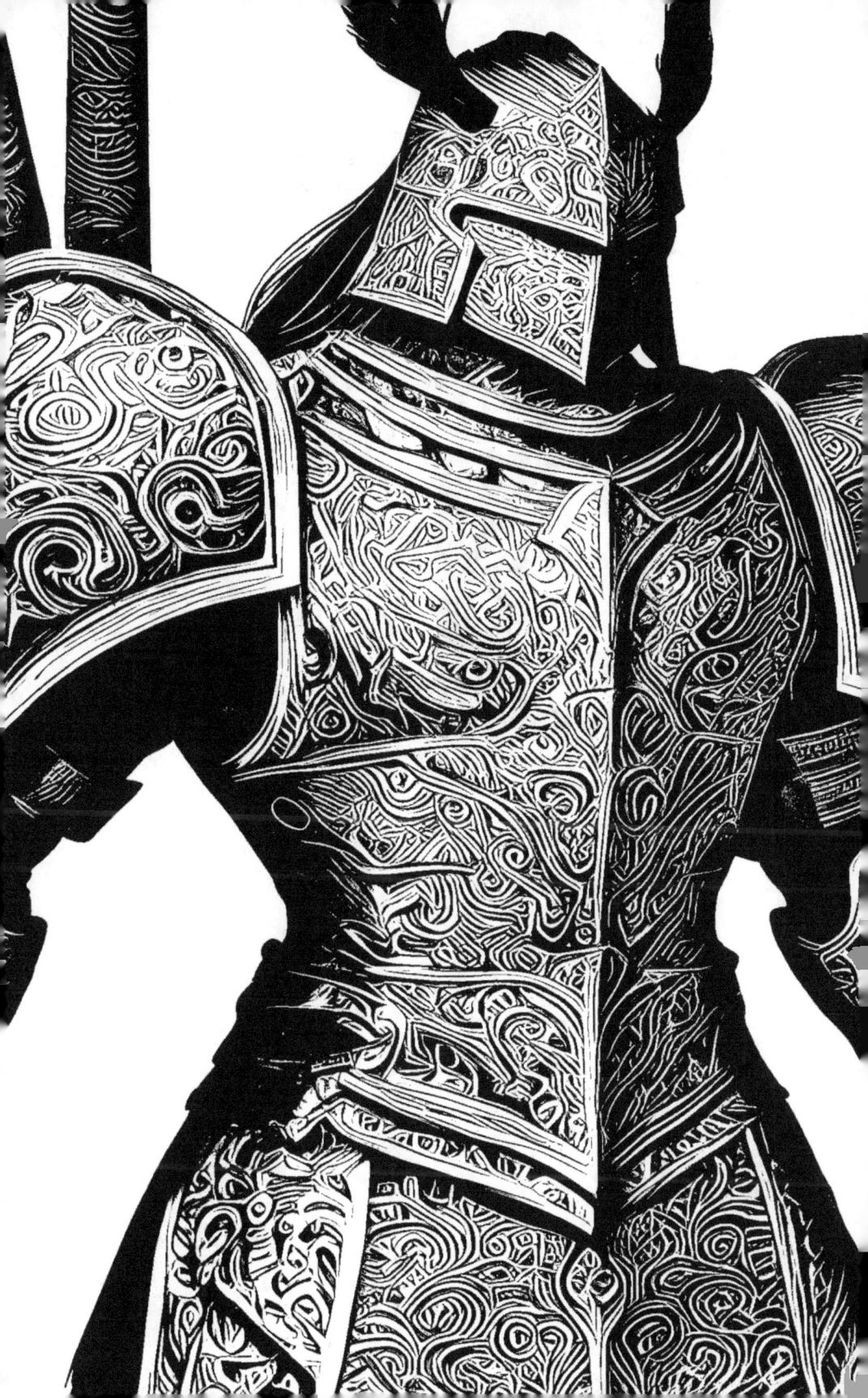

jeremyburt@ishopdailyonline.com jburt_01@hotmail.com
Make Money Online: https://ishopdailyonline.com
Print On Demand: https://ishopdaily.redbubble.com
Print On Demand @ Etsy: https://ishopdailyonline.etsy.com
dj12mind Instrumental Music Albums: https://dj12mind.com
Affiliate Products: https://index.ishopdailyonline.com
Patreon: https://www.patreon.com/user?u=80194438
Facebook: https://www.facebook.com/jeremy.burt2
Youtube:
https://www.youtube.com/channel/UCwV3nApPDh3dNHUGIX4w5nA
tiktok: https://www.tiktok.com/@jeremyburt4?lang=en
amazon: https://www.amazon.com/author/jeremyburt
THANK YOU FOR CHECKING IT OUT!

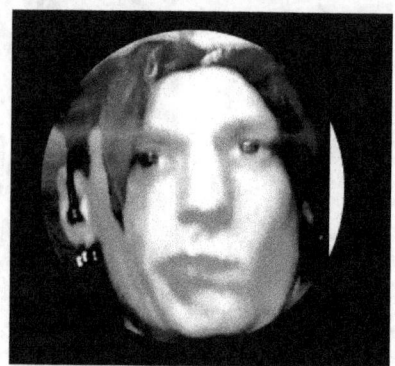